Dreams in Chinese Fiction

This book considers the contemporary political formula of the "Chinese Dream" in the light of the treatment of dreams in Chinese literary history since antiquity. Sinic literary and philosophical texts document an extensive spectrum of dream possibilities: starting with Zhuangzi's eminent butterfly dream, an early example of the inversion of the dreamer's reality, through to confusing visions of the spiritual realm. In classical dramas, novels, and ghost stories, dreams see the earthly realm enter into conflict with higher realms of existence. They indulge the dreamer's quest for sensual pleasures, but then supernatural beings relentlessly harvest the dreamers' life energy. Dreams promise spiritual enlightenment – only to abandon the dreamer in a state of utter confusion. In the early twentieth century, traditional dream knowledge is abandoned in favour or Freudian episodes of sexual repression. In this context, the collective national dream emerges as an unexpected vehicle of the pained individual's hope for national rejuvenation.

Johannes D. Kaminski is a scholar of comparative literature, interested in the literature of Chinese modernism, German classicism, and global science fiction. He is a SASPRO2-Fellow at the Institute of World Literature, Slovak Academy of Sciences. He is the author of *Lives and Deaths of Werther: Interpretation, Translation and Adaptation in Europe and East Asia* (2023).

Routledge Focus on Literature

Contemporary Irish Masculinities
Male Homosociality in Sally Rooney's Novels
Angelos Bollas

Creative Writing and the Experiences of Others
Strategies for Outsiders
Nandita Dinesh

Emotionality
Heterosexual Love and Emotional Development in Popular Romance
Eirini Arvanitaki

Digital Culture and the Hermeneutic Tradition
Suspicion, Trust, and Dialogue
Inge van de Ven and Lucie Chateau

Dreams in Chinese Fiction
Spiritism, Aestheticism, and Nationalism
Johannes D. Kaminski

Remapping Energopolitics
Blue Humanities, Geophilosophy and Sri Lankan Minor Writings
Abhisek Ghosal

For more information about this series, please visit: www.routledge.com/Routledge-Focus-on-Literature/book-series/RFLT

Dreams in Chinese Fiction
Spiritism, Aestheticism, and Nationalism

Johannes D. Kaminski

NEW YORK AND LONDON

First published 2025
by Routledge
605 Third Avenue, New York, NY 10158

and by Routledge
4 Park Square, Milton Park, Abingdon, Oxon, OX14 4RN

Routledge is an imprint of the Taylor & Francis Group, an informa business

© 2025 Johannes D. Kaminski

The right of Johannes D. Kaminski to be identified as author of this work has been asserted in accordance with sections 77 and 78 of the Copyright, Designs and Patents Act 1988.

All rights reserved. No part of this book may be reprinted or reproduced or utilised in any form or by any electronic, mechanical, or other means, now known or hereafter invented, including photocopying and recording, or in any information storage or retrieval system, without permission in writing from the publishers.

Trademark notice: Product or corporate names may be trademarks or registered trademarks, and are used only for identification and explanation without intent to infringe.

Library of Congress Cataloging-in-Publication Data
Names: Kaminski, Johannes Daniel, author.
Title: Dreams in Chinese fiction : spiritism, aestheticism, and nationalism / Johannes D. Kaminski.
Description: New York, NY : Routledge, 2025. |
Series: Routledge focus on literature |
Includes bibliographical references and index.
Identifiers: LCCN 2024010972 (print) | LCCN 2024010973 (ebook) |
Subjects: LCSH: Chinese fiction–HIstory and criticism. |
Dreams in literature. | Dreams–China.
Classification: LCC PL2419.D74 K36 2025 (print) |
LCC PL2419.D74 (ebook) | DDC 895.13009–dc23/eng/20240409
LC record available at https://lccn.loc.gov/2024010972
LC ebook record available at https://lccn.loc.gov/2024010973

ISBN: 9781032772172 (hbk)
ISBN: 9781032772196 (pbk)
ISBN: 9781003481881 (ebk)

DOI: 10.4324/9781003481881

Typeset in Times New Roman
by Newgen Publishing UK

Contents

List of figures	vi
Preface	vii
1 Philosophical foundations	1
2 Supernatural dream encounters	17
3 Tales of the strange	43
4 Erotic dreams	64
5 Collective national dreams	90
Index	*112*

Figures

1.1 Steep Ravines and Flying Cascades by Wu Bin (detail). Ink on paper, Song dynasty. National Palace Museum (Taipei). Licensed under CC BY 4.0   10

2.1 Liniang's Dream by an unknown master (detail). Woodcut print, Ming dynasty. In: *Die Rückkehr der Seele: Ein Romantisches Drama von Tang Hsiän Dsu*, 2 vols (Zurich: Rascher, 1937), I, 85. Image from the author's own copy   25

3.1 Bakemono no e by an unknown master (detail). Coloured ink on paper, Edo period. Brigham Young University, Tom Perry Special Collections. Reproduced with kind permission   56

4.1 Weiyang Sheng's Meditation Interrupted by Erotic Dreams by an unknown master (detail). Woodcut print on paper, Qing period. In: Li Yü, *Jou Pu Tuan: Ein erotisch-moralischer Roman aus der Ming-Zeit* (Braunschweig: Die Waage, 1965), 543. Image from the author's own copy   67

5.1 Dragon Boat Race by the Baojin Hall by Wang Zhenpeng (detail). Ink on paper, Yuan dynasty. National Palace Museum (Taipei). Licensed under CC BY 4.0   96

Preface

In March 2013, I spent several months in Beijing as a visiting scholar. My aim was to immerse myself in the *Dream of the Red Chamber*, an eighteenth-century novel replete with scenes of tender feelings and interpersonal brutality. The text is famed for blurring the boundaries between reality and fantasy. Baoyu, the protagonist, does not only experience life-changing dreams involving worried ancestors and seductive fairies, but the whole text is also framed as a dream, advancing a grand Daoist vision of cosmic instability that boils down to the enigmatic formula: 'When dreams become true, then truth becomes a dream.'[1] First, the protagonists' colourful lives suggest that the formula contains a life-affirming message, but as the plot progresses and their carefree youth yields to tragedy, the formula attains an escapist dimension, evoking a strong sense that all human aspirations are futile. Believing that such dream metaphors were an exclusive product of a literati culture of the past, I was little prepared to see dreams incorporated into national propaganda in twenty-first century China.

As I started to explore my neighbourhood, I saw every other wall freshly painted with slogans relating to the 'Chinese Dream of National Rejuvenation.' Across the road, there were billboards illustrating said Chinese Dream with ink drawings: humble fishermen going about their everyday life, solitary figures standing atop of mountains, resting travellers contemplating waterfalls. The Chinese Dream, I assumed, provided a counterweight against modernity, as decades of runaway economic growth have alienated the population from its historical past. Perhaps my studies of *Dream of the Red Chamber*, which colleagues of mine had previously dismissed as an escapist pastime, bore some relevance for the healing process that seemed to be playing out in this country. Obviously, I was wrong. When I started to add newspapers to my language studies, I came across invocations of the Chinese Dream that belied my naive assumptions, with headlines striking a decidedly nationalistic tone. Against the background of the country's territorial disputes with Japan over the Diaoyu (or Senkaku) Islands, with Beijing's growing impatience with Hong Kong's autonomy, and the prospect of a hot war over Taiwan, the invocations of national strength sounded daunting. In combination with the rhetoric of dreaming, a largely irrational act, I felt alarmed.

I sought out a professor of literature about the significance of those slogans, but he only took a deep drag of his cigarette, shrugged his shoulders, and scoffed: 'It's just empty words, forget about it. Nobody takes it seriously.' Back then, Xi Jinping had just become the General Secretary of the Chinese Communist Party. Being more known as the husband of a famous folk-singer, Peng Lihuan, than as a visionary politician at that time, he started to advance his own ideological agenda, even at the price of sounding outright silly. At least those were the professor's implications. His theory about the ideological vacuity seemed vindicated when pop culture adopted the term – for example when the local branch of the *Idol* franchise, a reality-television song contest, promoted the show under the name *The Sound of the Chinese Dream*.[2] This trend extended to academia, where political science scholars started to churn out dream-themed papers. The same played out in literary criticism, as researchers like me found themselves invited to conferences vaguely titled 'The Chinese Dream – Literature Dream.'[3]

As the years passed, Xi centralized and personalized power to a degree not seen since Mao Zedong. Today, as Xi's speeches, decrees, and writings are promoted as the highest evolution of statecraft and wisdom, dream-themed propaganda can no longer be ignored. Despite the vagueness of those formulations, observers cannot help to note that Xi's favourite metaphor is awkwardly rooted in the Chinese cultural nexus, where the dream sphere is endowed with greater dignity than elsewhere. This is in contrast to the West, where dreams may have opened the gates to metaphysical insights in the past – think of the dreams of Abraham, Jacob, and Constantine – but which have seen their relevance reduced to purely private affairs since the advent of modernity. Even the American Dream, the conceptual predecessor of the Chinese Dream, puts personal aspirations in the foreground rather than a shared vision of the nation's prosperity and glory.[4]

In 2012, the newly appointed General Secretary vaguely declared that 'realizing the great rejuvenation of the Chinese nation is the greatest dream of the Chinese nation since modern times.'[5] On the occasion of the CCP's centenary in 2021, Xi reiterated the claim that the party was leading the people towards 'the most magnificent chapter in the millennia-long history of the Chinese nation.'[6] Xi suggests that his Chinese Dream runs much deeper than twenty-first century geopolitics. In response to the omnipresence and unashamed vagueness of the concept, scholars have produced a plethora of studies on this subject. This applies to researchers from Chinese universities,[7] but also to their colleagues outside the People's Republic, who usually strike a more critical tone.[8] But this is not the place to elaborate on the exact meaning of Xi's Chinese Dream. Here, I wish to pursue a different path. This book takes the prominence of dream parlance in contemporary Chinese politics as an opportunity to explore and reexamine the abundant representations of oneiric experiences in Chinese literature. Literary dreams indeed provide positive blueprints for visions of national glory, especially in early-twentieth-century utopian literature, but the greater part of literary dreams cannot be reconciled with sociopolitical concerns. Take *The Governor of Nanke*, a tale from the eighth century CE, which tells of a dismissed military officer who falls asleep and dreams vividly of his ascendency as a mighty political ruler. Upon waking up, the sudden collapse of his spectacular dream biography leaves him so shocked that he becomes a monk.

One could certainly argue that speaking of 'dreams' in general terms is misleading. After all, one cannot compare the political rhetoric of dreams to the visions we have during sleep, let alone to their literary representation. The nocturnal prophetic visions experienced by ancient rulers have little in common with sexual dreams that lead to nocturnal emissions, a hotly debated area of concern in Chinese medical alchemy. Furthermore, there are literary dreams that do not exceed a character's personal horizon – let's call them natural dreams – and those that allow a protagonist to understand the workings of the world. Nevertheless, all of these different forms of dreaming fall under *meng* 夢, the Chinese term for 'dreams' and 'dreaming.' In the history of the language, *meng* always designated two related meanings: darkness of the senses and the act of dreaming.[9] The writers of the late imperial era established another usage when they titled their fictional texts *meng*, thereby emphasizing the proximity of dreaming and human creativity itself. In very general terms, the Chinese concept of *meng* implies that different kinds of reality exist in the shadows of the ordinary world, a plane of existence that destabilizes – and nurtures – the human world.

Next to accounts of Xi's Chinese Dream, scholarship has produced a wealth of studies on how dreams were – and in some cases continue to be – interpreted in the Sinic realm.[10] Emphasizing their incompatibility with modern ideas of the human psyche, medical scholars concluded that Chinese accounts of dreams sound 'absurd for contemporary researchers.'[11] One study even presses the point that the worldviews reflected in traditional oneirology are incompatible with modern egalitarian values.[12] In contrast to such presentist assessments, the field of literary studies has arguably broached the subject with greater nuance, as it elucidates the dream scenes in novels, dramas, and other genres not only in the light of physiological assumptions and metaphysical beliefs, but also with regards to narrative conventions. The following studies can be considered exemplary: the monograph by Lynn Struve, who traces the increase of literary dream discourse during the Ming dynasty, the study by Ling Hon Lam, who traces dream journeys in dramatic art, and the book by Qiancheng Li, who connects the dream motif in narrative fiction to their underlying Buddhist convictions.[13] Moving beyond the horizon of imperial China, David Der-wei Wang's and Lorenzo Andolfatto's studies investigate dreams in modern utopian and dystopian fiction, where spiritual or psychological depth is abandoned in favour of sociopolitical relevance.[14] Among translational enterprises, no other publication as done a greater service to the study of Chinese dreamscapes than Richard E. Strassberg's English translation of Chen Shiyuan's *Lofty Principles of Dream Interpretation*, a sixteenth-century text that compiles different theories to explain the medical, spiritual, and psychological meaning of a wide range of dreams.

While dreams are also the site of intense battles over interpretation in the occidental tradition,[15] the argument has been repeatedly made that a specific 'Chinese dream culture'[16] exists. The French journal *Extrême-Orient Extrême-Occident* widened this claim to include the other two great East Asian cultures, devoting a special issue to 'that East-Asian – Chinese, Korean and Japanese – sensibility toward dreams.'[17] On the one hand, to claim a special cultural proficiency in dreaming risks reproducing the distorted image of 'China as the Other', which Zhang Longxi so convincingly traced in poststructuralist thought, notably in Michel Foucault's preface to *The Order of Things* and Jacques Derrida's *Of Grammatology*.[18] On the other hand, to speak of a specifically Chinese kind of dreaming also reaffirms Xi's assertion of the nation's cultural uniqueness. Since this small book is not the right place to discuss the problems of area studies in a postcolonial and globalized world, this study exhibits little interest in producing comprehensive statements and essentializing judgements to either affirm or challenge existing preconceptions. Instead, the aim is to collect dream accounts with respect to specific topics, thereby granting textual sources enough room to speak for themselves. Perhaps, Juan Luis Borges, the Argentinian surrealist writer, can serve as an example to navigate Chinese literary dreamscapes. Taking note of the oneiric virtuosity of *Dream of the Red Chamber*, Borges observed that their impact was connected to a very specific narratological trick: 'The dreams [...] are more intense because the writer does not tell us that they are being dreamed, and so we think that they represent realities – until the dreamer awakes.'[19] Could it be that this idea of a 'Chinese dream culture' results more often from such literary devices rather than cultural factors?

Overview and notes

To account for the epistemological generosity found in Chinese literature, I place the focus on dream episodes themselves, an approach that requires extensive quotations, either from existing translations or as original renderings from classical, vernacular, or modern Chinese. Next to the general introduction to philosophical concepts, I found that the occasional reference to physiological, sociopolitical, and narratological contexts helps to gain a better understanding.

Chapter 1 introduces several dreams that were written and compiled in Chinese antiquity. Most importantly, this includes Confucius' dream of the Duke of Zhou and the butterfly dream of the *Zhuangzi*. Both have inspired vastly different interpretations that have themselves acquired canonicity through the ages. **Chapter 2** shows how supernatural dreams interfere with the protagonists' lives in narrative texts dating from the late Ming and early Qing period, including *Plum in the Golden Vase* (1596–1620), *Peony Pavilion* (1598), *Romance of the Western Chamber* (13th c.), and *Dream of the Red Chamber* (1759/91). **Chapter 3** closes in on so-called 'tales of the strange', a genre that was remarkable fertile for the documentation of bizarre dreams. Covering three millennia, the genre's history shows a changing narrative focus, starting with *In Search of the Supernatural* (4th c. BCE) to *Extensive Records of the Taiping Era* (10th c. CE) through to Pu Songling's *Strange Tales from a Chinese Studio* (1766). **Chapter 4** puts erotic dreams on centre stage. While Li Yu's *Carnal Prayer Mat* (1693) and *Dream of the Red Chamber* discuss human sexuality in medical terms that are informed by traditional physiology, Yu Dafu's and Guo Moruo's novellas of the 1920s document the appropriation of the occidental guilt complex. Finally, **Chapter 5** discusses the genealogy of the collective national dream, which first appeared in utopian novels of the late Qing era, such as Liu E's *Travels of Lao Can* (1903–1904) and Wu Jianren's *New Story of the Stone* (1905/ 1908). This kind of literary dream remains in circulation in contemporary China and is exploited in Xi Jinping's Chinese Dream-concept in order to further consolidate his power. Meanwhile, Ma Jian's novel *China Dream* (2018) satirically criticizes the vision of a homogenized national consciousness.

In Chinese names, the surname comes before the given name. For consistency, the running text of this study sticks to the East Asian convention (for example 'Tang Xianzu' rather than 'Xianzu Tang'). Bibliographic information proceeds in the same fashion. This rule does not apply when the writer carries an East Asian surname and Western given names (Christine Tan) or if the referenced text was originally published in an American or European context ('Juwen Zhang'). For the sake of clarity, titles published in Chinese feature detailed bibliographical information. The author's name is given in Romanized script, followed by the original hanzi. Book titles and articles are referenced in English translation, followed by the original title in hanzi and Romanized transcription, for example: Cao Xueqin 曹雪芹, *Dream of the Red Chamber* (紅樓夢 Hong lou meng).

The chapters of this book were originally produced for a series of workshops organized by *Dream Cultures*, an ICLA Research Committee dedicated to the inquiry into the cultural and literary history of the dream. The author thanks Manfred Engel for his encouragement to pursue this research topic.

Notes

1 This is the author's free translation, in which the ambiguous term *jia* (假) is translated as 'dream.' The original, written in classical Chinese, allows for

a degree of translational freedom: '假作真時真亦假.' Cao Xueqin, *Dream of the Red Chamber* (orig. 紅樓夢) (Shanghai: Shanghai guji chubanshe, 2007), 8. Chi-Chen Wang translates the passage as: 'When the unreal is taken for the real, then the real becomes unreal.' Cao Xueqin, *Dream of the Red Chamber*, transl. by Chi-Chen Wang (New York: Doubleday Anchor, 1958), 7. Meanwhile, David Hawkes' translation adds a self-referential dimension: 'Truth become fiction when the fiction's true.' Cao Xueqin, *The Story of the Stone* (*Dream of the Red Chamber*), trans. by David Hawkes, 5 vols (London: Penguin, 1973–1986), I, 55. Henceforth quoted as DRC with numbers of volume and page.
2 The show, originally titled *Zhongguo meng zhi sheng* (中國夢之聲), premiered on Dragon TV in 2013.
3 Organized by the Propaganda Department of the Shaanxi Provincial Party Committee and the Shaanxi Provincial Writers Association, the conference took place in 2014 in Xi'an. Its original title was 'Zhongguo meng – wenxue meng' (中國夢-文學夢).
4 See Suisheng Zhao, *The Dragon Roars Back: Transformational Leaders and Dynamics of Chinese Foreign Policy* (Stanford: Stanford University Press, 2023), 83.
5 Orig. '每個人都有理想和追求，都有自己的夢想。現在，大家都在討論中國夢，我以為，實現中華民族偉大覆興，就是中華民族近代以來最偉大的夢想。' Anon., 'Ten Paragraphs by Xi Jinping that Define the Meaning of the Chinese Dream' (習近平這十段話定義中國夢內涵), *Xinhua News* 29.11.2017, Website: xinhuanet.com/politics/2017-11/29/c_1122031311.htm (last accessed 1 March 2023). Unless otherwise stated, all translations my own, J. K.
6 Xi Jinping, 'Speech at a Ceremony Marking the Centenary of the Communist Party of China', July 1 2021, *Xinhua*, Website: www.xinhuanet.com/english/special/2021-07/01/c_1310038244.htm (last accessed: 4 August 2023).
7 While it is impossible to survey the industry of Chinese Dream-themed scholarship in China, the following two articles give an idea of the academic political discourse in China. The arguments evince a strong tendency to paraphrase Xi's speeches. See Cheng Meidong (程美東) and Zhang Xuecheng (張學成), 'A Review of Current Research on the Chinese Dream' (當前'中國夢'研究評述), *Studies on Socialism with Chinese Characteristics* (中國特色社會主義研究) 2 (2013), 58–65; Ruan Zongze (阮宗澤), 'The Common Humanity: China's "World Dream"' (人類命運共同體:中國的'世界夢') *International Affairs* (國際問題研究) 1 (2016), 9–21.
8 William Callahan points at the ideological vacuum of the concept. See William A. Callahan, 'Identity and Security in China: The Negative Soft Power of the China Dream', *Politics* 35.3–4 (2015), 216–229. Meanwhile, Michelle Tsai finds that the concept illustrates China's struggle of identity

between modern statehood and imperial nostalgia. See Michelle Hui-Ju Tsai, 'The Chinese Dream: Chinese Capitalism and Identity Politics', *Asian Survey* 59.2 (2019), 223–245.

9 Han-dynasty dictionaries paraphrase *meng* as darkness, confusion or gloomy mood. The Shuowen Jiezi (說文解字) paraphrases the term as 'not bright' (不明 bu ming). See Entry to '*meng* 夢', *Han Dian* (漢典), Website: www.zdic.net/hans/梦 (last accessed 1 August 2023). This said, the ancient term for dreaming is the homonym *meng* 寢. The character features the radical for wood, thus indicating the presence of a bed. Yet early narrative accounts soon ignored this distinction and also used the character *meng* 夢 to designate the mental activity that occurs during sleep.

10 For a general account on the interpretation of dreams, see Jing Pei Fang and Juwen Zhang, *The Interpretation of Dreams in Chinese Culture* (Trumbull: Weatherhill 2000), 20. For a special consideration of the period between Qin and Han dynasties, see Fu Zhenggu (傅正谷), *History of Chinese Dream Literature* (中國夢文學史) (Beijing: Guangming ribao chubanshe, 1993). For studies of the late imperial era, see Michael Lackner, *Der chinesische Traumwald: Traditionelle Theorien des Traums und seiner Deutung im Spiegel der ming-zeitlichen Anthologie 'Meng-lin hsüan-chieh'* (Frankfurt am Main: Peter Lang, 1985); Marion Eggert, *Rede vom Traum: Traumauffassungen der Literatenschicht im späten kaiserlichen China* (Stuttgart: Steiner, 1993); Wai-Yee Li, 'Dreams of Interpretation in Early Chinese Historical and Philosophical Writings', in: *Dream Cultures: Explorations in the Comparative History of Dreaming*, ed. by David Shulman and Guy G. Stroumsa (New York: Oxford University Press, 1999), 17–42.

11 See Calvin Kai-Ching Yu, 'The Yellow Emperor's Canon of Internal Medicine and the Interpretation of Typical Dreams Two Millennia Ago', *Dreaming* 26.3 (2016), 250–269, here 266.

12 Closing in on the traditional medical frameworks that connect specific dreams to pathology, Hsiu-fen Chen identifies the norms of a patriarchal society, in which non-reproducing women have no place. See Hsiu-fen Chen, 'Between Passion and Repression: Medical Views of Demon Dreams, Demonic Fetuses, and Female Sexual Madness in Late Imperial China', *Late Imperial China* 32.1 (2011), 51–82.

13 See Lynn A. Struve, *The Dreaming Mind and the End of the Ming World* (Honolulu: University of Hawai'i Press, 2019); Ling Hon Lam, 'The Peony Pavillion: Emotions, Dreams, and Spectatorship', in: *How to Read Chinese Drama: A Guided Anthology*, ed. by Patricia Sieber and Regina Llamas (New York: Columbia University Press, 2022), 212–234; Qiancheng Li, *Fictions of Enlightenment: Journey to the West, Tower of Myriad Mirrors and Dream of the Red Chamber* (Honolulu, University of Hawai'i Press, 2004).

14 See David Der-wei Wang, 'Utopian Dream and Dark Consciousness: Chinese Literature at the Millennial Turn', *Prism* 16.1 (2019), 136–156; Lorenzo Andolfatto, *Hundred Days' Literature: Chinese Utopian Fiction at the End of Empire, 1902–1910* (Leiden: Brill, 2019).
15 For a general account that considers the interplay between dreams and literature, see Otto M. Rheinschmiedt, *The Fiction of Dreams: Dreams, Literature, and Writing* (London: Taylor and Francis, 2018).
16 See Richard E. Strassberg, 'Introduction', in: *Wandering Spirits: Chen Shiyuan's Lofty Principles of Dream Interpretation* (Berkeley: University of California Press, 2008), i–xvi, here i.
17 Orig. 'cette sensibilité est-asiatique – chinoise, coréenne, japonaise – aux rêves.' Vincent Durand-Dastès and Rainier Lanselle, 'Le récit de rêve en Asie orientale: langues et genres', *Extrême-Orient Extrême-Occident* 42.1 (2018), 5–14, here 8.
18 See Longxi Zhang, 'The Myth of the Other: China in the Eyes of the West', *Critical Inquiry* 15.1 (1988), 108–131.
19 Orig. 'Los sueños […] son más intensos porque el escritor no nos dice que los están soñando y creemos que se trata de realidades, hasta que el soñador se despierta.' Jorge Luis Borges, *Textos cautivos* (Madrid: Alianza, 1998), 343.

Bibliography

Andolfatto, Lorenzo. *Hundred Days' Literature: Chinese Utopian Fiction at the End of Empire, 1902–1910* (Leiden: Brill, 2019).
Anon. 'Ten Paragraphs by Xi Jinping that Define the Meaning of the Chinese Dream' (習近平這十段話定義中國夢內涵), *Xinhua News* 29.11.2017, Website: xinhuanet.com/politics/2017-11/29/c_1122031311.htm (last accessed 1 March 2023)
Borges, Jorge Luis. *Textos cautivos* (Madrid: Alianza, 1998).
Callahan, William A. 'Identity and Security in China: The Negative Soft Power of the China Dream', *Politics* 35.3–4 (2015), 216–229.
Cao, Xueqin. *Dream of the Red Chamber*, trans. by Chi-Chen Wang (New York: Doubleday Anchor, 1958).
———. *The Story of the Stone* (*Dream of the Red Chamber*), trans. by David Hawkes, 5 vols (London: Penguin, 1973–1986).
———. *Dream of the Red Chamber* (orig. 紅樓夢) (Shanghai: Shanghai guji chubanshe, 2007).
Chen, Hsiu-fen. 'Between Passion and Repression: Medical Views of Demon Dreams, Demonic Fetuses, and Female Sexual Madness in Late Imperial China', *Late Imperial China* 32.1 (2011), 51–82.
Cheng, Meidong (程美東) and Zhang Xuecheng 張學成. 'A Review of Current Research on the Chinese Dream' (當前 '中國夢' 研究評述), *Studies*

on *Socialism with Chinese Characteristics* (中國特色社會主義研究) 2 (2013), 58–65.
Durand-Dastès, Vincent and Rainier Lanselle (eds.). *Extrême-Orient Extrême-Occident* 42.1 (2018).
Eggert, Marion. *Rede vom Traum: Traumauffassungen der Literatenschicht im späten kaiserlichen China* (Stuttgart: Steiner, 1993).
Fang, Jing Pei and Juwen Zhang. *The Interpretation of Dreams in Chinese Culture* (Trumbull: Weatherhill, 2000).
Fu, Zhenggu (傅正谷). *History of Chinese Dream Literature* (中國夢文學史) (Beijing: Guangming ribao chubanshe, 1993).
Lackner, Michael. *Der chinesische Traumwald: Traditionelle Theorien des Traums und seiner Deutung im Spiegel der ming-zeitlichen Anthologie 'Meng-lin hsüan-chieh'* (Frankfurt am Main: Peter Lang, 1985).
Lam, Ling Hon. 'The Peony Pavillion: Emotions, Dreams, and Spectatorship', in: *How to Read Chinese Drama: A Guided Anthology*, ed. by Patricia Sieber and Regina Llamas (New York: Columbia University Press, 2022), 212–234.
Li, Qiancheng. *Fictions of Enlightenment: Journey to the West, Tower of Myriad Mirrors and Dream of the Red Chamber* (Honolulu, University of Hawai'i Press, 2004).
Li, Wai-Yee. 'Dreams of Interpretation in Early Chinese Historical and Philosophical Writings', in: *Dream Cultures: Explorations in the Comparative History of Dreaming*, ed. by David Shulman and Guy G. Stroumsa (New York: Oxford UP, 1999), 17–42.
Rheinschmiedt, Otto M. *The Fiction of Dreams: Dreams, Literature, and Writing* (London: Taylor and Francis, 2018).
Ruan, Zongze (阮宗澤). 'The Common Humanity: China's "World Dream"' (人類命運共同體:中國的'世界夢') *International Affairs* (國際問題研究) 1 (2016), 9–21.
Strassberg, Richard E. *Wandering Spirits: Chen Shiyuan's Lofty Principles of Dream Interpretation* (Berkeley: University of California Press, 2008).
Struve, Lynn A. *The Dreaming Mind and the End of the Ming World* (Honolulu: University of Hawai'i Press, 2019).
Tsai, Michelle Hui-Ju. 'The Chinese Dream: Chinese Capitalism and Identity Politics', *Asian Survey* 59.2 (2019), 223–245.
Wang, David Der-wei. 'Utopian Dream and Dark Consciousness: Chinese Literature at the Millennial Turn', *Prism* 16.1 (2019), 136–156.
Xi, Jinping. 'Speech at a Ceremony Marking the Centenary of the Communist Party of China', July 1 2021, *Xinhua*, Website: www.xinhuanet.com/english/special/2021-07/01/c_1310038244.htm (last accessed: 4 August 2023)
Yu, Calvin Kai-Ching. 'The Yellow Emperor's Canon of Internal Medicine and the Interpretation of Typical Dreams Two Millennia Ago', *Dreaming* 26.3 (2016), 250–269.

Zhang, Longxi. 'The Myth of the Other: China in the Eyes of the West', *Critical Inquiry* 15.1 (1988), 108–131.

Zhao, Suisheng. *The Dragon Roars Back: Transformational Leaders and Dynamics of Chinese Foreign Policy* (Stanford: Stanford University Press, 2023).

1 Philosophical foundations

The shocking discontinuity between dreaming and waking represents a fundamental experience shared by members of different cultures across time. With dreamers perplexed by the sudden disconnection between the two realms, cultural reference systems provide guidance and help individuals manoeuvre the overlapping boundaries between dreamscapes and waking consciousness. This short overview of the foundations of Chinese oneirology centres on six iconic dreams, which were written and compiled during the extended period of turmoil that coincided with the collapsing Zhou dynasty (1046–256 BCE). As thinkers hoped to rectify the ills of their present, they also drew on dreams, hoping to establish a meaningful connection with a glorified past ruled by wise men. These dreams acquired canonicity in the centuries and millennia following their compilation. In consideration of the literary dreams discussed in the following chapters, this survey puts forward a small philosophic corpus to assess conceptual borrowings and instances of artistic license. This survey concentrates on historical commentary, very much at the expense of modern thought, which has also paid considerable attention to those dreams independently of interpretative traditions.

In Chinese antiquity, dreams were assigned a variety of functions. In one classification, for example, there are (1) quotidian dreams with natural causes, be they physiological or psychological; (2) those indicating an interaction between the dreamer and spirits; and (3) 'strange' ones, such as dreams of dreaming.[1] This chapter addresses the latter two categories: ancestral dreams, oneiric journeys that facilitate encounters with time-transcending authorities, and strange dreams that initiate spiritual awakening. During the earliest dynasties,

DOI: 10.4324/9781003481881-1

2 Philosophical foundations

divination played a central role in statecraft, from using oracle bones, a technique that includes carving questions into tortoise shells and consulting the *Book of Changes* (易經 Yi jing) (1000–750 BCE), to the interpretation of dreams proper. Needless to say, interpreting dreams through the *Book of Changes* remains widely popular up until today, especially among Sinic populations and New Age enthusiasts. Long before commoners gained access to arcana, however, non-quotidian, prophecy-worthy dreams were primarily assigned to people of high social rank.

The *Classic of Poetry* (詩經 Shi jing, 11th to 7th c. BCE), a collection of the earliest Chinese poetry in circulation, features a hymn that tells of a dream prophecy made to a king. After consolidating his power, he oversees the construction of a magnificent palace that not only protects him from wind and rain, but also offers the comfort required for good sleep a homely atmosphere. It is not until long afterwards that he has a prophetic dream:

> Comfortably he sleeps,
> He sleeps and wakes
> And interprets his dreams.
> 'Your lucky dreams, what were they?'
> 'They were of black bears and brown,
> Of [lizards] and snakes.'
> The diviner thus interprets it:
> 'Black bears and brown
> Mean men-children.
> Snakes and [lizards]
> Mean girl-children.'
> So he bears a son,
> And puts him to sleep upon a bed,
> Clothes him in robes [...].
> Then he bears a daughter,
> And puts her upon the ground,
> Clothes her in swaddling-clothes[.][2]

In the original, this scene is presented in four-character lines that evince a strong sense of symmetry, thereby reiterating the idea that the dream symbols directly correspond to their decoded messages.[3] The king's dream is interpreted twice, first by the dreamer himself who instantly classifies his vision as 'lucky,' then by the mancer who provides more detail. During the early Zhou dynasty (1046–771 BC), such great importance was attributed to dreams that the rank of the Director of Divination (太卜 taibu) was conceived, whose primary task consisted of interpreting the dreamlife of the ruling family, a task that would offer important insight into the country's future.[4] Although this office also presented ample opportunity for the Director of Divination to abuse his power, the overall method of interpretation was based on the principles that underly Chinese philosophy and medicine at large, using a set of correlations that are typical for Chinese cosmology. To dream of strong animals such as bears, for example, indicates the prevalence of *yang* (陽) energy, the active force of the cosmos, which also determines the gender of the embryo during pregnancy. Meanwhile, to dream of supposedly weak animals like snakes and lizards indicates *yin* (陰) energy, designating the birth of female offspring.[5]

Compared with the mancer's interpretation of the king's dream, other prophetic dreams strike a more prescriptive tone, especially those dreams chronicled in the *Records of the Grand Historian* (史記 Shi ji). This applies to Duke Wen's dream of 'a yellow serpent dangling down from heaven and touching the ground'[6], a vision that is decoded as the command to build a sacrificial altar. Prophecy also comes in handy when rulers need advice. In this vein, Wu Ding, an ancient emperor of the Shang dynasty (12th c. BC), is said to have consulted his dreams when looking out for the best people to become his ministers. After the Supreme Deity answers his call, Wu Ding has a portrait made of the man he saw in his dream and initiates an empire-wide search for an individual with matching features. Eventually, they find Fu Yue, a humble construction worker, who finds himself swiftly promoted to the inner circle of the emperor. To anticipate excessively superstitious interpretation of Wu Ding's dream, Neo-Confucian commentators like the Cheng brothers (Cheng Hao 1032–1085 and Cheng Yi 1033–1107) emphasized the *li*-dimension (理) of this episode. Conceived as the ontological foundation of all things,[7] *li* presupposes the synchronicity of the king's dream and the actual existence of Fu Yue:

> If Fu Yue had not been a man of virtues, he would not have been able to respond to Gaozong's telepathic call. It is like divining. [...] If the words in the books do not conform to the principles, the divination will not come true, of course.[8]

4 Philosophical foundations

Evidently, such strong belief in the benefits of divination also came with drawbacks. Emperor Huizong (1083–1135), for example, allowed fortune-tellers to have the final say on important placements, much to the critique of subsequent historians who could not help relating this habit to his promotion of incompetent personnel and to his many military defeats.[9]

Confucianism, a dominant cultural force from the second century BC onwards, does not dispense with this ambivalent approach to the oneiric, in which mythological and spiritual elements coexist. In contrast to the often-repeated claim that Confucianism is a rationalistic religion devoid of any magic belief,[10] Confucius himself contributed to the canonical status of divination texts such as *Book of Changes* by issuing lengthy commentary on all hexagrams. In the *Analects* (論語 Lun yu), a collection of the sage's teachings dating from the 2nd century BCE,[11] one passage merits special attention in view of the ambivalent status of dreams as a means of enlightenment. The following dream report exhibits a strongly spiritistic innuendo that subsequent Confucian commentators were eager to dispel: 'How seriously I have declined! It has been so long since I last dreamt of meeting the Duke of Zhou.'[12] Confucius refers to the semi-legendary ruler (11th c. BCE), famed for combining political sagacity with cultural achievements.[13] Given Confucius' self-conception as a mere transmitter of ancient teachings, dreaming of the Duke was interpreted as signalling total immersion while the absence of such dreams indicates a lack of dedication. Consequently, commentators such as Lü Buwei, the author of *Spring and Autumn Annals* 呂氏春秋 (*Lüshi chunqiu*, 239 BC), considered Confucius's statement as the invocation of an ideal state of mind: 'With this sort of intensely focused will, what task could they [Confucius and Mozi] not master? what action could they not bring to completion? [...] Of course, [this] is not a result of the spirits actually reporting to you, but of your focus and total immersion.'[14] After all, the natural cause for such dreams lies not in a supernatural visitation, but in one's preoccupation with intense study. After such scepticism already featured in the core classics of Confucian literature, following generations of scholars continued their attacks on superstitious beliefs, including Xie Zhaozhe (1567–1624), who declared: 'I emphatically disbelieve dreams. Of all the fortunes and misfortunes of my whole life, not one has been [foretold] in a dream. I thus know they do not bear credence.'[15]

Philosophical foundations 5

Given the prominence of Confucius's dream of the Duke of Zhou, humorous writing also gladly picked up on this episode to ridicule the pretences of scholars who hide their laziness behind a veil of learned references:

> A teacher dozes off during class hours in broad daylight. When he wakes up he makes up a story, 'I was dreaming of the Duke of Zhou.' The next day the student also dozes off during the class. The teacher strikes him with a ferule and scolds him, 'How could you fall asleep?' The student says, 'I, too, was dreaming of the Duke of Zhou.' The teacher challenges him, 'Oh, really? What did the Duke of Zhou say?' 'He said he did not see you yesterday', answers the student.[16]

In contrast to secular interpretations of Confucius's dream, the proliferation of spiritual beliefs in China also allowed for the dream's literal interpretation, supposing that the Duke had indeed previously visited the sage. Zhu Xi (1130–1200), one of the principal thinkers of Neo-Confucianism, established that encounters with the dead are indeed possible; after all, people 'contain the remaining *qi* [氣] of their ancestors.'[17] On the same account, the passage of the *Analects* also contributed to Duke of Zhou's installation as a 'dream god' in folkloristic belief, a deity who notifies people of important events through dreams. Once dream interpretation became common among the population, the legendary Duke was also attributed the authorship of the *Duke of Zhou's Interpretation of Dreams* (周公解夢 Zhou Gong jiemeng, c. 7th century BCE), an anonymous text that offers interpretations of dream motifs. Here, dream symbols are considered non-psychological, prophetic keys for future events. In contrast to the kind of work of interpretation that centred around the king's family, this book is directed at a general audience, as dream motifs are assigned either auspicious or infelicitous meaning.[18] This text's popularity is still undiminished today.

No account of Chinese dreams would be complete without the butterfly dream of the *Zhuangzi* (莊子), a collection of parables, fables, and anecdotes dating from the 4th to 2nd centuries BCE, which revolve around Zhuangzi, a legendary sage.[19] This dream report exemplifies the quintessential 'strange' dream:

> Once Zhuang Zhou dreamed he was a butterfly, a butterfly flitting and fluttering around, happy with himself and doing as he pleased.

He didn't know he was Zhuang Zhou. Suddenly he woke up, and there he was, solid and unmistakable Zhuang Zhou. But he didn't know if he were Zhuang Zhou who had dreamed he was a butterfly or a butterfly dreaming he was Zhuang Zhou. Between Zhuang Zhou and a butterfly, there must be some distinction! This is called the Transformation of Things [物化 wuhua].[20]

This account upsets the neat distinction between dreamer and dream. After all, the immersion into a dream and waking up from one are analogous experiences: in both cases, the environment of the dreaming subject is exchanged for another. The enigmatic nature of the text also required commentators to offer concise answers to two ambiguous elements: can Zhuang Zhou be identified with the narrator? What significance does the 'Transformations of Things' (物化 wuhua) possess, a terminological borrowing from the *Dao De Jing* (道德經, 4th c. BCE)?

As one of the most important editors of *Zhuangzi*, Guo Xiang (252–312 CE) established an interpretation that infers that the narrator, who observes the scene from a 'zero-perspective,'[21] should be distinguished from Zhuang Zhou. As the subject who is undergoing the transformation, he is unaware of what is happening to him, which also implies that no memories exist that can bridge across the two forms of experience:

> His not being aware of being a butterfly now is no different from his not being aware of being Zhuang Zhou while he was dreaming. However, since each state suited him comfortably at the time, there is no way to be sure that he was not a butterfly now dreaming that he was Zhuang Zhou. It commonly happens in the world that someone takes a nap and dreams the experiences of a lifetime, so there is no way to be sure that one's present lifetime is not just something dreamed during a nap.[22]

For Guo Xiang, the insight that the butterfly is as real as Zhuang Zhou has a considerable implication for human existence: 'The distinction between being awake and dreaming is no different than the distinction between life and death.'[23] Consequently, one would be ill-advised to worry about death, a state of being that is phenomenologically disconnected from being alive. Another parable of the *Zhuangzi* illustrates this indifferent attitude to life with the sage's reaction to his wife's passing, as he reminds himself that her death was effected by the same forces that contributed to her birth: 'It's just like the progression of the four seasons: spring, summer, fall, winter.'[24] According to scholarship, Guo Xiang's line of interpretation encourages humans to yield to incessant change, as the invoked Transformations of Things (物化 wuhua) 'means entering the next phase of existence, in this case, what we ordinarily call "death." '[25]

Hanshan Deqing (1546–1623), a Buddhist commentator, pursued a different approach to the butterfly dream. Crediting the sages Zhuangzi and Confucius with considerable insight into the karmic cycle, he argued that their texts guide the reader towards a higher awareness. According to this syncretist approach, the *Zhuangzi* documents the transcendence of ordinary consciousness, leading to insights that only a great sage of the future will be able to verify.[26] In view of the narrative perspective, Hanshan infers the unity between Zhuang Zhou and the narrator. In this case, the reported dream experience has a direct effect on the dreamer's spiritual wakening:

> In order to realize one's original true governor [真宰 zhen zai], one must forget the 'I' [忘我 wang wo]. And primary in the spiritual effort to forget the 'I' is to gaze upon the secular world as though it were a dream, upon disputes over right and wrong as things in a dream, and upon those who [attempt to] correct such disputes as performing dream divinations within a dream. If one uses 'dream' to contemplate the secular world, then ideas of [other] people [vis-à-vis] oneself will likewise naturally dissolve. [...] In case one can see the falseness of [the bodily] 'I' but cannot forget things, [Zhuang Zhou deploys] the likes of the butterfly-dream parable so that things and self are both forgotten. When things and self are both forgotten, then right and wrong disappear.[27]

The decisive difference between Guo's and Hanshan's interpretations lies in the latter's basic assumption that a 'withdrawal from the world' (出世 chushi) is possible. After learning that life is but a dream, Zhuang Zhou can free himself from the constraints of earthly life. Indeed, many Western translations of the butterfly dream, such as Herbert Giles's and Martin Buber's, emphasize this soteriological aspect.[28] Meanwhile, according to a truly Daoist worldview, the ideal of observing an indifferent attitude to life is unrelated to the hope for transcendence, as constant change results from an instable but immanent cosmos.

8 Philosophical foundations

Despite their differences with regard to the dreamer's hopes to see through the veil of illusion, both interpretations of the butterfly dream support the pedestrian view of Daoism as a strand of thought that pursues escapism at the expense of active involvement in statecraft. This is not necessarily a valid observation. Another Daoist classic, the *Liezi* (列子 4th c. BCE), features a ruler's dream that stands on par with Confucius's dreams of the Duke of Zhou and Wu Ding's nightly vision of his future minister. Here, the legendary Yellow Emperor is introduced as an imperfect ruler who only gradually achieved supreme insight. After having exhaustingly devoted himself to the pleasures of life, he starts to worry about his empire's misgovernment. But his sudden attention to state matters only makes things worse, so he eventually gives up and retreats from political life. The following dream account departs from the narrative brevity observed in the previous examples:

> [The Yellow Emperor] retired to live undisturbed in a hut in his main courtyard, where he fasted to discipline mind and body, and for three months had nothing to do with affairs of state.
>
> Falling asleep in the daytime, he dreamed that he was wandering in the country of [Huaxu]. This country is to the West of [Yan] province in the far West, to the North of [Tai] province in the far North West, who knows how many thousands and myriads of miles from the Middle Kingdom. It is a place which you cannot reach by boat or carriage or on foot, only by a journey of the spirit. In this country there are no teachers and leaders; all things follow their natural course. The people have no cravings and lusts; all men follow their natural course. They are incapable of delighting in life or hating death, and therefore none of them dies before his time. [...] They go into the water without drowning, into fire without burning; hack them, flog them, there is no wound nor pain; poke them, scratch them, there is no ache nor itch. They ride space as though walking the solid earth, sleep on the void as though on their beds; clouds and mist do not hinder their sight, thunder does not confuse their hearing, beauty and ugliness do not disturb their hearts, mountains and valleys do not trip their feet – for they make only journeys of the spirit.
>
> When the Yellow Emperor woke, he was delighted to have found himself. He summoned his ministers [Tianlao], [Limu] and [Taishan Chi], and told them:

'I have lived undisturbed for three months, fasting to discipline mind and body, and meditating a way to care for myself and govern others, but I did not find a method. Worn out, I fell asleep, and this is what I dreamed. Now I know that the utmost Way cannot be sought through the passions. I know it, I have found it, but I cannot tell it to you.'

After another twenty-eight years, when the Empire was almost as well governed as the country of [Huaxu], the Emperor rose into the sky. The people did not stop wailing for him for more than two hundred years.[29]

The Yellow Emperor's detailed account is divided into four parts: following the observation that the empire is misgoverned, the ruler makes several attempts to act against this deficit until a dream vision sends him to the mythical land of Huaxu to witness the complete unity between the Dao and the human sphere. Finally, the Emperor returns to the waking world, equipped with the secret of good governance. This unmistakably Daoist take on the perfect state of nature centres around an ideal that Philip Ivanhoe has characterized as 'unselfconsciousness.'[30] Untainted by self-concern, individuals and society at large can achieve a state of complete indifference toward joy and – perhaps more importantly – pain. One of the most striking aspects of this vision is the absence of teachers and leaders among its people. This allows for two interpretations: was this state of perfection achieved by a wise ruler, who disappeared after guiding the country on the right track? Or was this state achieved by the absence of teachers and leaders? Perhaps, such questions are secondary; after all, the supernatural acts performed by the people of Huaxu, such as invulnerability and flying, indicate that the Yellow Emperor's task lies less on applying Huaxu's standards to the world of men but in the correct translation of its principles. Therefore, the main lesson remains concealed from the reader, who must figure out how the Emperor transformed his empire to become 'almost as well governed as the country of [Huaxu]' before transforming into an immortal himself. Given the prominence of philosophical journeys into fantastical lands, Chinese landscape painting used such references to explore visual representation of impossible landscapes that host enlightened communities (see Figure 1.1).

10 *Philosophical foundations*

Figure 1.1 Steep Ravines and Flying Cascades by Wu Bin (detail). Ink on paper, Song dynasty. National Palace Museum (Taipei). Licensed under CC BY 4.0.

Conclusion

All the above examples infer that the oneiric realm facilitates communication between the world of humans and Heaven (天 tian), one of the central metaphysical concepts of Chinese philosophy. Imagined as an anthropomorphic entity that has awareness, preferences, and values, Heaven grants the Mandate of Heaven (天命 tianming) to shield society – and its rulers – against the forces of disintegration and destruction.[31] While the prophetic dream facilitates insights in the workings of faith, the oneiric interventions seen in Wu Ding's, Confucius,' and the Yellow Emperor's cases offer instructions on correct rule and behaviour in general. Heaven also plays an important role in Zhuang Zhou's dream, as it represents the cosmic force that drives the Transformation of Things. That being said, the discussed strands of dream interpretation advance different ideas about how Heaven interacts with men, as one and the same dream gave rise to vastly incompatible readings: the Duke of Zhou, the paragon of Confucian virtue, transformed into a dream god; and the *Zhuangzi*'s butterfly, a Daoist emblem of incessant change, became emblematic of Buddhist self-realization. Evidently, the distinctions between the three traditional metaphysical systems of China cannot be drawn so sharply. Written in an anecdotal style, these dream reports exemplify an important aspect of early Chinese philosophy. Located at the intersection between historical writing and philosophical argumentation, they move beyond the normative power of denotative speech because their authors 'were not horrified by the prospect that the past could be understood to have multifarious and divergent meanings'[32], as Paul van Els and Sarah Queen point out. In this respect, Chinese philosophical writing already features a narrative quality that challenges modern assumptions about how to distinguish between discursive writing and fiction.

In the following chapters, literary accounts use prophetic, soteriological, and enigmatic dreams to frame the narrative, tell of extraordinary events, and make a case for sociopolitical visions. Often enough, they also seize the opportunity to ridicule classical accounts and to self-consciously relate the act of dreaming to the act of writing itself.

Notes

1 See Jing Pei Fang and Juwen Zhang, *The Interpretation of Dreams in Chinese Culture* (Trumbull: Weatherhill, 2000), 20.
2 Confucius (孔子) (ed.), *The Book of Songs*, trans. by Arthur Waley (New York: Grove, 1960), 283–284. With small amendments by the author.
3 The poem 'Si gan' (斯干), often translated as 'Building', forms part of the Lesser Court Hymns (小雅 xiao ya), which were composed during the 8th and 9th century BCE. The original reads: '吉夢維何，維熊維羆，維虺維蛇。大人占之，維熊維羆，男子之祥。維虺維蛇，女子之祥。' Gao Heng 高亨, *Annotated Classic of Poetry* (詩經今注 Gao Heng Shijing jinzhu) (Shanghai: Shanghai guji chubanshe, 1980), 265.
4 See Sakade Yoshinobu, 'Divination as a Daoist Practice', in: *Daoism Handbook*, ed. by Livia Kohn (Leiden: Brill, 2000), 541–566.
5 This interpretation is derived from Xiong Bolong (熊伯龍, 1617–1669), a scholar who rejects this kind of interpretation, as he finds that 'the dreams of pregnant women are not all like this.' Quoted in: Lynn A. Struve, *The Dreaming Mind and the End of the Ming World* (Honolulu: University of Hawai'i Press, 2019), 51.
6 Sima Qian (司馬遷), *Records of the Grand Historian of China*, trans. by Burton Watson, 2 vols (New York: Columbia University Press, 1961), II, 17
7 See Siu-chi Huang, *Essentials of Neo-Confucianism* (London: Greenwood, 1999), 87.
8 Quoted in: Yu Chang and Deyuan Huang, 'The Spirit of the School of Principles in Zhu Xi's Discussion of *Dreams* and on *Confucius did not Dream of Duke Zhou*', *Frontiers of Philosophy in China* 5 (2010), 94–110, here 97.
9 See Wang Zengyu, 'Witchcraft and Divination', in: *A Social History of Middle-Period China*, ed. by Zhu Ruixin et al. (Cambridge: Cambridge University Press, 1998), 431–446, here 435; Patricia Ebrey, 'Taoism and the Art at the Court of Song Huizong', in: *Taoism and the Arts of China*, ed. by Stephen Little et al. (Chicago: Art Institute, 2000), 96–112, here 96.
10 The appreciation of Confucianism as a rational religion was first advanced by Leibniz's *Novissima Sinica*, allowing anti-clerical rationalists to align themselves with Confucianism. See Franklin Perkins, 'Leibniz on the Existence of Philosophy in China', in: *China in the German Enlightenment*, ed. by Daniel Leonhard Purdy and Bettina Brandt (Toronto: University of Toronto Press, 2016), 60–79. The idea of Confucianism's rational outlook on the world remains firmly in place. See Xinzhong Yao, *An Introduction to Confucianism* (Cambridge: Cambridge University Press, 2000), 47.
11 Confucius's *Analects* have a complex editorial history. While three versions coexisted in the Han dynasty, the text that was canonized dates

from the mid-Han Dynasty. It was written by several authors, who wrote during the three centuries after Confucius's death (551–479 BCE). See Amy Olberding, 'Introduction', in: *Dao Companion to the* Analects, ed. by A. O. (Dordrecht: Springer, 2014), 1–20, 2.
12 Confucius (孔子), *Analects: With Selections from Traditional Commentaries*, trans. by Edward Slingerland (Cambridge, MA: Hackett, 2003), 65.
13 Today, the Duke of Zhou's idealized status is considered the product of 'a willfully misremembered past.' Scott Cook, 'Confucius and the Zhou Dynasty', in: *Oxford Handbook of Confucianism*, ed. by Jennifer Oldstone-Moore (Oxford: Oxford University Press, 2023), 70–83, here 76. This said, contemporary Chinese philosophy, notably Zhao Tingyang's thought, continues to draw on the Zhou dynasty as a time-transcending model of politics. See Zhao Tingyang, *All under Heaven: The Tianxia System for a Possible World Order*, trans. by Joseph E. Harroff (Berkeley: University of California Press, 2021).
14 Lü Buwei (呂不韋), *The Annals of Lü Buwei*, trans. by John Knoblock and Jeffrey Riegel (Stanford: Stanford University Press, 2000), 618.
15 Quoted in: Struve, *The Dreaming Mind*, 51.
16 Quoted in: Hsu Pi-ching, *Feng Menglong's Treasury of Laughs: A Seventeenth-Century Anthology of Traditional Chinese Humour* (Leiden: Brill, 2015), 71.
17 Quoted in: Chang and Huang, 'The Spirit', 98.
18 The manual features intuitive, counterintuitive, and seemingly random interpretations of dream symbols. Dreams of walking with a woman, for example, indicate a loss of wealth, while dreams of sitting with a woman foretell good fortune. See Duke of Zhou (周公), *The Duke of Zhou's Interpretation of Dreams*, trans. by Nikita Bushin (Beijing: Purple Cloud Press, 2021), 62.
19 The text's genesis remains a topic of scholarly debate and speculation. See Esther Sunkyung Klein, 'Early Chinese Textual Culture and the *Zhuangzi* Anthology: An Alternative Model for Authorship', in: *Dao Companion to the Philosophy of the Zhuangzi*, ed. by Kim-chong Chong (Cham: Springer, 2022), 13–42.
20 Zhuangzi (莊子), *The Complete Works*, trans. by Burton Watson (New York: Columbia University Press, 2013), 18.
21 See Hans-Georg Möller, 'Zhuangzi's "Dream of the Butterfly": A Daoist Interpretation', *Philosophy East and West* 49.4 (1999), 439–450, here 445.
22 Quoted and translated in: Christine Abigail Lee Tan, *Freedom as Self-realization:* Zide *in the Neo-Daoist Philosophy of Guo Xiang*, Doctoral thesis Nanyang Technological University (Singapore) 2020, DOI: https://doi.org/10.32657/10356/148932, 150–151.
23 Quoted in: Tan, *Freedom*, 151.

14 *Philosophical foundations*

24 Zhuangzi, *The Complete Works*, 191.
25 Masayuki Sato, 'The Multi-level Structure of "Transformation" and the Philosophy of "Transformation of Things" in the Zhuangzi', in: *Dao Companion to the Philosophy of the Zhuangzi*, ed. by Kim-chong Chong (Cham: Springer, 2022), 135–162, here 144.
26 See Struve, *The Dreaming Mind*, 95.
27 Quoted in: Struve, *Dreams End of Ming*, 96.
28 See Herbert Giles, *Chuang Tzu: Mystic, Moralist, and Social Reformer* (London: B. Quaritch, 1889); Martin Buber, *Reden und Gleichnisse des Tschuang-Tse* (Leipzig: Insel, 1910).
29 Liezi (列子), *The Book of Lieh-tzu*, trans. by A. C. Graham (New York: Grove, 1960), 34–35.
30 See Philip J. Ivanhoe, 'The Theme of Unselfconsciousness in the Liezi', in: *Riding the Wind with Liezi: New Perspectives on the Daoist Classic*, ed. by Ronnie Littlejohn and Jeffrey Dippmann (New York: State University of New York Press, 2011), 127–150.
31 See Franklin Perkins, 'Metaphysics in Chinese Philosophy', in: *The Stanford Encyclopedia of Philosophy* (last revision 24 May 2019), ed. by Edward N. Zalta, Website: https://plato-stanford-edu.uaccess.univie.ac.at/entries/chinese-metaphysics/ (last accessed 27 July 2023).
32 Paul van Els and Sarah A. Queen, 'Introduction', in: *Between History and Philosophy: Anecdotes in Early China*, ed. by P. v. E. and S. A. Q. (Albany: State University of New York Press, 2017), 1–38, here 18.

Bibliography

Buber, Martin. *Reden und Gleichnisse des Tschuang-Tse* (Leipzig: Insel, 1910).
Chang, Yu and Deyuan Huang. 'The Spirit of the School of Principles in Zhu Xi's Discussion of *Dreams* and on *Confucius did not Dream of Duke Zhou*', *Frontiers of Philosophy in China* 5 (2010), 94–110.
Confucius (孔子). *Analects: With Selections from Traditional Commentaries*, trans. by Edward Slingerland (Cambridge, MA: Hackett, 2003).
——— (ed.). *The Book of Songs*, trans. by Arthur Waley (New York: Grove, 1960).
Cook, Scott. 'Confucius and the Zhou Dynasty', in: *Oxford Handbook of Confucianism*, ed. by Jennifer Oldstone-Moore (Oxford: Oxford University Press, 2023), 70–83.
Duke of Zhou (周公). *The Duke of Zhou's Interpretation of Dreams*, trans. by Nikita Bushin (Beijing: Purple Cloud Press, 2021).
Ebrey, Patricia. 'Taoism and the Art at the Court of Song Huizong', in: *Taoism and the Arts of China*, ed. by Stephen Little et al. (Chicago: Art Institute, 2000), 96–112.
Fang, Jing Pei and Juwen Zhang. *The Interpretation of Dreams in Chinese Culture* (Trumbull: Weatherhill, 2000).

Gao, Heng (高亨). *Annotated Classic of Poetry* (詩經今注 Gao Heng Shijing jinzhu) (Shanghai: Shanghai guji chubanshe, 1980).

Giles, Herbert. *Chuang Tzu: Mystic, Moralist, and Social Reformer* (London: B. Quaritch, 1889).

Huang, Siu-chi. *Essentials of Neo-Confucianism* (London: Greenwood, 1999).

Ivanhoe, Philip J. 'The Theme of Unselfconsciousness in the Liezi', in: *Riding the Wind with Liezi: New Perspectives on the Daoist Classic*, ed. by Ronnie Littlejohn and Jeffrey Dippmann (New York: State University of New York Press, 2011), 127–150.

Klein, Esther Sunkyung. 'Early Chinese Textual Culture and the *Zhuangzi* Anthology: An Alternative Model for Authorship', in: *Dao Companion to the Philosophy of the Zhuangzi*, ed. by Kim-chong Chong (Cham: Springer, 2022), 13–42.

Liezi (列子). *The Book of Lieh-tzu*, trans. by A. C. Graham (New York: Grove, 1960).

Lü, Buwei (呂不韋). *The Annals of Lü Buwei*, trans. by John Knoblock and Jeffrey Riegel (Stanford: Stanford University Press, 2000).

Möller, Hans-Georg. 'Zhuangzi's "Dream of the Butterfly": A Daoist Interpretation', *Philosophy East and West* 49.4 (1999), 439–450.

Olberding, Amy (ed.). *Dao Companion to the Analects* (Dordrecht: Springer, 2014).

Perkins, Franklin. 'Leibniz on the Existence of Philosophy in China', in: *China in the German Enlightenment*, ed. by Daniel Leonhard Purdy and Bettina Brandt (Toronto: University of Toronto Press, 2016), 60–79.

———. 'Metaphysics in Chinese Philosophy', in: *The Stanford Encyclopedia of Philosophy* (last revision 24 May 2019), ed. by Edward N. Zalta, Website: https://plato-stanford-edu.uaccess.univie.ac.at/entries/chinese-metaphysics/ (last accessed 27 July 2023)

Sakade, Yoshinobu. 'Divination as a Daoist Practice', in: *Daoism Handbook*, ed. by Livia Kohn (Leiden: Brill, 2000), 541–566.

Sato, Masayuki. 'The Multi-level Structure of "Transformation" and the Philosophy of "Transformation of Things" in the Zhuangzi', in: *Dao Companion to the Philosophy of the Zhuangzi*, ed. by Kim-chong Chong (Cham: Springer, 2022), 135–162.

Sima, Qian (司馬遷). *Records of the Grand Historian of China*, trans. by Burton Watson, 2 vols (New York: Columbia University Press, 1961).

Struve, Lynn A. *The Dreaming Mind and the End of the Ming World* (Honolulu: University of Hawai'i Press, 2019).

Tan, Christine Abigail Lee. Freedom as Self-realization: *Zide* in the Neo-Daosit Philosophy of Guo Xiang, Doctoral thesis Nanyang Technological University (Singapore) 2020, DOI: https://doi.org/10.32657/10356/148932

van Els, Paul and Sarah A. Queen (eds.). *Between History and Philosophy: Anecdotes in Early China* (Albany: State University of New York Press, 2017).

Yao, Xinzhong. *An Introduction to Confucianism* (Cambridge: Cambridge University Press, 2000).
Zengyu, Wang. 'Witchcraft and Divination', in: *A Social History of Middle-Period China*, ed. by Zhu Ruixin et al. (Cambridge: Cambridge University Press, 1998), 431–446.
Zhao, Tingyang (趙汀陽). *All under Heaven: The Tianxia System for a Possible World Order*, trans. by Joseph E. Harroff (Berkeley: University of California Press, 2021).
Zhuangzi (莊子). *The Complete Works*, trans. by Burton Watson (New York: Columbia University Press, 2013).

2 Supernatural dream encounters

In Chinese history, literary merit and popular appeal were often disjointed categories, as the command of the Five Classics required readers to master a language that was accessible only to a small elite, Classical Chinese. As a consequence, much of the written language diverged substantially from the vernacular and the many dialects that were used across the Sinosphere. This said, premodern narrative texts succeeded in crafting a literary language that not only features clever references to the Classsics, but also allowed narrators and fictional characters to use everyday, even vulgar language. Furthermore, such texts indulged in metaphysical speculations and freely adapted orthodox concepts to great dramatic effect. During the Yuan period (c. 1270 to 1368 CE), dramatists coined an aesthetic approach which remained relevant until the end of Qing dynasty (1644 to 1911). This combination of supranatural and realist elements met the approval of literary commentators and censors while also appealing to larger audiences. Following Yuan drama, the budding prose genre of *xiaoshuo* also embraced this combination.

This chapter focusses on a selection of premodern texts concerned with dreams. Instead of following a strictly chronological order, the material is arranged thematically and moves from examples of spiritism to philosophic visions. In the first text, *Plum in the Golden Vase* (金瓶梅 Jin ping mei, 1596–1620), dreams have a comparatively limited function: they facilitate communication with people who have passed away. In the second, *Peony Pavilion* (牡丹亭 Mu dan ting, 1598), the protagonist's dream allows for an encounter with her destined lover. Further dissociating the dreamscape from the earthly realm, *Romance of the Western Chamber* (牡丹亭 Mu dan ting, 13th c.) features a soteriological dream intended to enlighten the protagonist. Finally, in *Dream of the Red Chamber* (紅樓夢 Hong lou meng, 1759/1792[1]), dreams are assigned such a powerful position within the narrative that they dwarf the protagonists' earthly lives.

Communication with the dead in *Plum in the Golden Vase*

Plum in the Golden Vase belongs to the literary category of *xiaoshuo* (小說), a genre that shows notable similarities to the European novel. This said, the anonymity of its author, its sprawling outline, its sexual explicitness, and its concern for karmic retribution indicate a marked difference to the bourgeois novel.[2] Despite the text's epic scope – David T. Roy's full translation runs to approximately 2700 pages – Andrew H. Plaks finds that *Plum in the Golden Vase* 'projects a sense of unity of conception virtually unparalleled in the early history of colloquial Chinese fiction.'[3] Plaks sees this unity implemented primarily by structural composition, parallelisms, and rhetoric. One can also convincingly argue that dreams hold the key to an overarching narrative that tells of crime and punishment.

At the beginning of the narrative stands a crime which would remain unnoticed if it were not for a dream. Pan Jinlian, a sensual and deceitful woman, and Ximen Qing, a wealthy merchant, engage in a passionate affair and figure out a way to do away with Jinlian's husband. Because they slowly poison him day by day, nobody becomes suspicious of their crime, except for the husband's younger brother, Wu Song. Upon returning from a long journey, he is surprised to hear of his brother's burial and Jinlian's quick re-marriage to Ximen. Wu Song contacts his brother's spirit to clarify the cause of his premature death. He asks him for a revelatory dream:

> A little after the first watch Wu [Song] lit the incense, prostrated himself, and kowtowed, saying: 'Elder Brother, hear me, if your departed soul be not too far away! When you were in this world you were of a meek disposition, and now that you are dead the circumstances remain unclear. Look you, if you have
>
> > Suffered injustice and harbour resentment,[4]
>
> as the victim of a murder, appear to me in a dream. As your brother I will undertake to:
>
> > Requite your wrong and assuage your resentment.'
>
> Pouring the wine to make a libation, and burning the paper money, Wu commenced to weep aloud, saying:

'After all
We came into this world by the same route.'
He wept to such effect that among the neighbours to either side there were none who were not moved. [...] It was around midnight and Wu:
Tossed first this way and then that,
but could not get to sleep. All he could do was to give vent to long sighs. His orderly, meanwhile, lay there, snoring away, stretched out as if he were a dead man. Wu got to his feet to look around and saw that the glass lamp on the table that held the spirit tablet seemed to be:
Half alight and half extinguished.
He sat down on the mat again [...]. [H]e suddenly became aware of a gust of cold wind swirling up from underneath the table that held the spirit tablet. Behold:
Devoid of shape and form,
Neither fog nor mist;
Swirling like an eerie wind,
its chill invades the bones; [...]
All too dimly, it conceals
the poison-eater's ghost [...].
This gust of cold wind made Wu's hair stand on end. When he took a close look, he saw someone climbing out from underneath the table that held the spirit tablet, who called out to him, 'Younger Brother, I died a grievous death!'[5]

Although the younger brother cannot tell the nature of this vision ('Was it a dream or not a dream?', PGV I, 179), it sufficiently establishes Jinlian and Ximen's guilt for him.

After the lustful couple continues its depraved lifestyle for some time, Wu Song eventually wreaks a terrible vengeance on Jinlian, as he storms her compound and kills her in a gruesome fashion. At this point, he finds their household in disarray: while Ximen has already died in Jinlian's arms after consuming too many potency-enhancing pills (chapter 79), the latter was making final preparations for eloping with Ximen's first-born son, good-for-nothing Chen Jingji. Her timely killing prevents them from continuing their quasi-incestuous relationship. Owing to the unfortunate discrepancy between the laws that govern the human and the spiritual spheres, Jinlian's soul is forced to roam about. While imperial regulations state that the bodies of murder victims cannot be buried as long as the perpetrator is at large, popular belief posits that souls are doomed to roam about as long as their bodies have not received the required ceremonial treatment. In this baneful situation, she visits Jingji, her last lover, in a dream to ask him a favour:

> At present, the Underworld will not admit me, so that, by day, I can only [d]rift aimlessly about; and, by night, I have to scrounge around everywhere in search of offerings made to the deceased. Just now, I received the hundred sheets of paper money that you burned for me, but that enemy of mine [i.e. Wu Song] has not yet been apprehended, and my corpse is lying in a temporary grave on the street. If you are still moved by our old feelings for each other, you might buy a coffin, put my corpse into it, and see that I am properly buried, so that I will not have to lie there exposed for days on end. (PGV V, 137)

Chen Jingji explains that he cannot follow his late lover's orders for fear of his other mother-in-law (Ximen's household is polygamous), then wakes up.

In both cases, in Wu Song's and in Jingji's dreams, the living are visited by the dead while in a dormant state, which corresponds to the folkloristic belief that dreams are vehicles of communication with one's ancestors. The idea that the dead are connected to their progeny through their *qi*, a point made by the Confucian philosopher Zhu Xi, accounts for both dream visitations. This is evident in Wu Song's case, who encounters his deceased brother, but also with regard to Jingji. Although he and Jinlian are not connected by a blood line, she is still his mother-in-law and, once dead, becomes part of his ancestry. According to folklore belief, however, there also exists a difference between respectable ancestor ghosts and spectres like Jinlian. Only as long as the deceased receive a proper burial and sacrifices can they join their ancestors; otherwise, they turn into haunting spirits (厲鬼 ligui) who haunt their kinsfolk and friends. And when people die a violent death, they may even transform into a licentious demon (淫厲 yinli).[6] According to one particular theory, these spirits are produced by the sun or the moon shining on unburied human remains, which accounts for the alchemic logics behind Jinlian's fate.[7]

Plum in the Golden Vase combines stylistic virtuosity with an unprecedented degree of explicitness. As public mores changed during the end of the Ming dynasty,[8] subsequent authors answered to the cultural significance of the text while, at the same time, providing a more rigid moral framework. Ding Yaokang's (1599–1669) text *Continuation of Plum in the Golden Vase* (續金瓶梅 Xu Jin ping mei, 1654) concentrates on the unintended consequences of obscene reveries.[9] This extends to the punishment of a young girl, Jingui, who keeps dreaming of a sexual encounter that is modelled after the grape arbour scene, the *Plum in the Golden Vase*'s most graphic description of intercourse.[10] In a dream, Jingui meets a man dressed in a moon-white silk gown:

> As they held hands, their tongues tasted each other's fragrant saliva. Intoxicated by wine, they nurtured their desire. Jingui could not control herself und took off her undergarment. They proceeded to the grape arbour, under which he spread her thighs and tied them to the roof. Now they could enjoy themselves without restraint. The man in the white clothes took out a purple thing large as an eggplant. He slowly applied saliva to it and inserted it into Jingui's hole. This excited her extraordinarily, and, all of a sudden, her juices started dripping everywhere. She only took notice of the man undoing his silk gown and taking her under the canopy. Then Jingui lost her senses.
>
> Suddenly, she heard the cock-crow. The man in the white silk gown was gone. Outside Jingui's doorstep, Meiyu could be heard saying: 'My girl has been resting for days, I shouldn't have come.'[11]

Despite the scene's explicitness, its hurried description and lack of detail marks a clear departure from the original. Following her sudden awakening, the narrator interrupts the story to explain that Jingui's dream was not an innocent, inconsequential fantasy. In fact, an evil spirit exploited Jingui's weakness: 'Since the lecherous act under the grape arbour was repeated today, the evil spirit could exploit her weakness by taking on the shape of Ximen and by absorbing his soul. As she dispersed her juices, her vitality suffered great damage. During daytime, she started to talk in confusion, she also could no longer take food and fell gravely ill for ten days.'[12] Eventually she becomes infertile.

It should be pointed out that her dreaming does not entail sinfulness, a concept that is alien to the Confucian system and folklore. Jingui's failure to occupy her mind with proper thoughts during the daytime results in her physiological degradation rather than the damnation of her soul. The implicit recommendation is that prudent individuals should strive to dream of the Duke of Zhou rather than of carnal dalliance.

Lovers' dreams in *Peony Pavillion*

The romantic drama *Peony Pavilion* also demonstrates the failure of a young girl's self-discipline. In contrast to *Continuation to Plum in the Golden Vase*, however, the dreaming maiden is rewarded rather than punished. Tang Xianzu's (1550–1616) lengthy play – a full production would take 20 hours – revolves around an unlikely love story, which the original preface summarizes succinctly:

> Dreaming of a lover [Du Liniang] fell sick; once sick she became ever worse; and finally, after painting her own portrait as a legacy to the world, she died. Dead for three years, still she was able to live again when in the dark underworld her quest for the object of her dream was fulfilled.[13]

At the beginning of the drama, Liniang lives in isolation with her father, her mother, and a servant girl. Since the father, Du Bao, worries about her inclination to daydream, an old Confucian scholar is employed to teach her the Classics. In the first lesson, they go through the first lines of the *Classic of Poetry*:

> *Guanguan* cry the ospreys
> on the islet in the river.
> So delicate the virtuous maiden,
> a fit mate for our Prince. (PP 25)

These lines nourish the young girl's imagination with a series of sensual images. She soon complains: 'Heaven, now I begin to realize how disturbing the spring's splendour can be. They were all telling the truth, those poems and ballads I read' (PP 45).[14] By radically identifying with the mating metaphors in the text, Liniang emulates a reading technique proposed by Mencius (372–289 BC), the other principal founding father of Confucianism: to trace back the original intention of the author with one's sympathetic understanding (以意逆志 yi yi ni zhi).[15] Mencius' concern for reconstructing authorial intention established the idea that all literature and especially poetry must be understood as deeply personal utterances by their authors.[16] Employing her 'sympathetic understanding' to understand these lines, Liniang's attention is drawn to the glorious springtime outside her window.

Seeking solace in the spring garden adjacent to the family compound, she finds herself overwhelmed by sensual impressions and falls asleep in a pavilion. The internalized lines of the *Shijing* trigger an erotic dream:

> (*She falls asleep and begins to dream of Liu Mengmei, who enters bearing a branch of willow in his hand.*)[17]

LIU MENGMEI:
 As song of oriole purls in warmth of sun,
 so smiling lips open to greet romance.
 Tracing my path by petals borne on stream,
 I find the Peach Blossom Source of my desire.
I came along this way with Miss Du – how is it that she is not with me now? (*He looks behind him and sees her*) Ah, Miss Du!

> (*She rises, startled from sleep, and greets him. He continues*)

So this is where you were – I was looking for you everywhere. (*She glances shyly at him, but does not speak*) I just chanced to break off this branch from a weeping willow in the garden. You are so deeply versed in works of literature, I should like you to compose a poem to honor it.

> (*She starts in surprised delight and opens her lips to speak, but checks herself*)

[LINIANG] *(aside):* I have never seen this young man in my life – what is he doing here?
LIU *(smiling at her):* Lady, I am dying of love for you!
 With the flowering of your beauty
 as the river of years rolls past,
 everywhere I have searched for you
 pining secluded in your chamber.
Lady, come with me just over there where we can talk.

> (*She gives him a shy smile, but refuses to move.*
> *He tries to draw her by the sleeve*)
>
> [LINIANG] *(in a low voice):* Where do you mean?
> LIU:
>
> > There, just beyond this railing peony-lined
> > against the mound of weathered Taihu rocks.
>
> [LINIANG] *(in a low voice):* But, sir, what do you mean to do?
> LIU *(also in a low voice):*
>
> > Open the fastening at your neck
> > loose the girdle at your waist,
> > while you
> > screening your eyes with your sleeve,
> > white teeth clenched on the fabric as if against pain,
> > bear with me patiently a while
> > then drift into gentle slumber
>
> (*[Liniang] turns away, blushing. Liu advances*
> *to take her in his arms, but she resists him*)
> LIU, [LINIANG]: Somewhere at some past time you and I met.
>
> > Now we behold each other in solemn awe
> > but do not say
> > in this lovely place we should meet and speak no word.
> >   (*Liu exits, carrying off [Liniang] by force.*) (PP 47–48)

Although not explicit like *Plum in the Golden Vase*, where genitals are named and described in great detail, this oneiric scene confidently represents the erotic tension between the protagonists (see Figure 2.1). The couple's low-voiced dialogue, the male lover's announcement of how he will undress the girl and her customary blushing lead up to the consummation of their love. While the dramatic action skips their sexual encounter, Liniang gives an account of what happened 'over there' in retrospect: 'he carried me to a spot beside the peony pavilion, beyond the railings lined with trees, peonies, and there together we found the "joys of cloud and rain"' (PP 51–52). This statement leaves nothing unsaid: the idiom of 'playing clouds and rain' (雲雨 yunyu) is the conventional metaphor for the sexual encounter.[18] Once awake, sixteen-year-old Liniang is haunted by this oneiric one-night stand, as she is overwhelmed by a feeling that her youth is going to waste. Despite her increasing agony, her father remains firm in his resolution

Figure 2.1 Liniang's Dream by an unknown master (detail). Woodcut print, Ming dynasty. In: *Die Rückkehr der Seele: Ein Romantisches Drama von Tang Hsiän Dsu*, 2 vols (Zurich: Rascher, 1937), I, 85. Image from the author's own copy.

not to marry her off until she has reached a certain age. Unable to exercise such restraint, she dies.

The play's central idea derives from the Chinese folklore belief in *yuanfen* (緣分), romantic fate, a power which operates beyond human control.[19] *Peony Pavilion* embraces this concept and adds a karmic dimension to this concept: if Liniang dies prematurely without having fulfilled her love destiny, she may as well get the chance to be resurrected from the dead. After Liniang's ghost reminds the Judge of Reincarnation that she never met the person who she was destined to love, she does voluntarily what Jinlian's uncoffined corpse was forced to do in agony: she roams around the world of the living as a ghost to find her lover.

The play's central mystery, how Liniang can dream of a lover she has never even laid eyes on, harks back to the passage in *Records of the Great Historian* in which emperor Wu Ding is looking to recruit the best people in the empire as his ministers, then dreams of Fu Yue, whom he swiftly promotes to his inner circle. In the drama, the law of *li* synchronicity is applied to the lovers: had Liniang not been destined for Liu Mengmei, she would not have dreamed of him. If their union would not conform to *yuanfen*, their encounter would not be possible. Since *yuanfen*, like *li*, is a dynamic principle, the lovers must still overcome manifold obstacles. After their initial dream encounter led to Liniang's premature death, the pair of lovers receives the opportunity to meet again, as Liu Mengmei, still ignorant of his love destiny, comes across the self-portrait that she painted prior to her death. He is immediately love-struck, even if he does not immediately identify the girl on the picture with the ghost who keeps slipping under his blankets night after night. Once she is able to convince him of her identity, he does not hesitate to dig up her corpse and bring her back to life, upon which her father accuses Liu of grave robbery. As it seems that the lovers' union is once again obstructed, the Emperor steps in. As the Son of Heavens, he eventually legitimizes 'that supremely deviant union of ghost and grave robber'[20] through declaring her a real human fit to be married to Liu Mengmei.

As in *Plum in the Golden* Vase, dreams in *Peony Pavilion* correspond to an intermediate realm inhabited by restless ghosts. In contrast to the story of Ximen Qing and Pan Jinlian, Liniang's ghost is not part of the dreamer's past but of his future life, as both Liu Mengmei and Liniang are drawn to each other – without having ever met.

Enlightening dreams in *Romance of the Western Chamber*

Wang Shifu's (or Wang Dexin, 13th c.) comic drama *Romance of the Western Chamber* pre-dates *Peony Pavilion*. The featured dream scene, however, only became central to the drama's interpretation in the wake of its critical reassessment during the 17th century – that is, during a time, when *Peony Pavilion* had assumed classical status despite its oneiric extravagance. Once again, this drama concentrates on the complications of coupling: Zhang Sheng, a romantic young scholar whose 'dreams never leave the shadows of willors or the shade of flowers'[21], and Cui Yingying, an over-protected maiden, fall in love with another. Even after Zhang Sheng saves her from being captured by bandits, he still meets the opposition of her mother, a pitiless widow, and falls sick. Intending to save him from dying of a broken heart, Yingying starts to pay him nightly visits until their illicit relationship is brought to light. Yingying's mother consents to their marriage, but only on one condition: Zhang Sheng must immediately depart for the capital and pass the imperial examination. Only then should the lovers be reunited.

On the first day of his voyage, Zhang Sheng stays the night at an inn thirty miles away from his departure point. After he falls asleep, Yingying appears to him in a dream:

[*YINGYING:*] He's in this inn. I'll have to knock on the gate.
[*ZHANG SHENG:*] Who's knocking? It's a girl's voice. I'll open the door and look. Who could it be at this time?
 If you are human, hurriedly declare yourself;
 If you are a ghost, disappear immediately!
[*YINGYING:*] It's me!
 The madam was sleeping, and I was thinking,
 Now he's gone, when will I see him again?
 So I came to go on with you.
 ([he] *sings*)
 Hearing this, I pull her by her fragrant silken sleeves[22] –
 So, it was you all the time!
 ([he] *speaks*) Missy, such ardour is hard to find.
 ([he] *sings*) Your character is such, you really give it your all.
 You haven't given a thought to your clothes:
 Your embroidered shoes have been stained by dew, water, and mud,
 And the soles of your feet ruined by walking.

[*YINGYING:*] It was all for you. I didn't care how far it was!
[*ZHANG SHENG sings*]:   I imagine how you neglected sleep and forgot to eat,
> Your perfume dissipating, your jade diminishing.
> 'Flowers open, flowers fall,'
> But I still feel that's off the mark –
> Rather: the pillow cold, the covers chilly;
> The phoenix alone, the simurgh[23] lonely;
> The moon so round by clouds obstructed.
> I conjure up what pain you must have felt.
> [*he sings to a different tune:*]
> A human life, I think, suffers most bitterly from separation.
> How touching! A thousand miles of passes and mountains
> You've traversed all alone.
> Could such soul-baring dedication
> Be rewarded with treacherous infidelity?
> Even though for a while the flower is tattered, the moon is incomplete,
> Don't ever think you'll be 'a sunken jug, a broken hairpin.'
> I don't fancy the high and mighty,
> Don't envy the proud and opulent.
> Alive, we'll share the same blanket;
> Dead, we'll share the same grave. (WW 249–251)

Despite the occasional reference to the possibility of abandoning her, Yingying's appearance strengthens his resolve to devote his life to her. As he revels in declarations of love, their night-time get-together is interrupted by the sudden arrival of soldiers. Yingying stays calm and confronts them confidently:

[*SOLDIERS*]: We saw a girl crossing the Yellow River a moment ago, but we don't know where she went. Bring a torch! It's clear that she's fled into this inn. Bring her out! Bring her out!

[*ZHANG SHENG*]: What do we do now?

[*YINGYING*]: You stand back. I'll open the gate myself and confront them.

> [*she sings*] Stubbornly you surround the [house], set to work with spades and picks;
> Cruelly, you grab our throats, pull out swords and axes.
> Rebellious hearts and gluttonous eyes are by nature deformed.

[ZHANG SHENG]: Let me confront them.

[Yingying sings]: Don't speak;
   Stand back.

[Soldier:] Whose daughter are you to cross the Yellow River in the dead of the night?

[YINGYING:] Don't talk nonsense.
   General Du [i.e. Zhang Sheng's protector] – you know him as a hero –
   He'll glance just once and turn you into salted pickles;
   He'll point just once and transform you into blubber and blood.
   He'll come riding a white horse!
      (*[Soldier] grabs [Yingying] and leaves.*)

[ZHANG SHENG:] Ai, so it was a dream all the time. Let me open the gate and look – all I see is a whole heaven of dewy vapor, a whole earth of frosty flowers. [...]
   Without reason swallow and magpie clamor on the highest branch;
   On a single pillow a dream of mandarin ducks fails to coalesce.
(WW 250)

The sight of magpies, messengers of love in Chinese poetry, fails to correspond to the sad reality he finds outside. Although the scene represents the protagonist's transition from waking to dreaming in a seamless manner, the oneiric nature of both the visitation and the assault is made evident; after all, Yingying's surprise visit and her eloquence are somewhat out of character and come quite as a surprise. In the final act, everything works out according to plan: Zhang Sheng passes the examination as primus and, after one last act of resistance on the part of her mother, is betrothed to his beloved. In the light of this happy ending, Zhang Sheng's dream can be interpreted along a rationalist framework. The natural cause behind his nightmare is of psychological origin: having said farewell to Yingying, he misses her and, in consideration of her earlier assault, fears for her safety.

Despite the drama's immense popularity during the Ming and Qing dynasties, it was considered a lewd book (邪書 xieshu) for its provocative views of love and the explicit depiction of the lovers' sexual encounters.[24] To challenge the book's status, Jin Shengtan (1608–1661), a Buddhist critic, attempted its rehabilitation as a quasi-Buddhist tale of renunciation. On the one hand, he highlights Yingying's moral virtue, arguing that she made love with Zhang Sheng not to satisfy her carnal desire, but out of a sense of compassion and duty. After all, she owes him a debt of gratitude for saving her from the bandits. On the other hand, he dismisses the fifth act, when Zhang Sheng and Yingying finally marry, as a mere addition by another author. This sanguine and life-affirming ending, argues Jin, conceals the play's hidden layer of meaning which revolves around Zhang Sheng's dream at the inn. Accordingly, this nightly vision allows Zhang to break out of the wheel of samsara (輪迴 lunhui). His awakening from the dream indicates his ultimate detachment from worldly cares.[25]

Far-fetched as it may seem, Jin's interpretation is partly legitimized by the original narrative on which *Western Chamber* is based. In *Story of Yingying* (鶯鶯傳 Yingying zhuan, 8th century), Zhang Sheng's departure initiates the couple's gradual alienation from one another. Eventually, both marry different partners. Considering this background story, his dream can be seen as a dramatic variant of this melancholic ending. Yingying's kidnapping foreshadows the dissolution of her bond with Zhang Sheng and her marriage to another man. Conversely, the fifth act serves as an ironic addition that adds a melancholic dimension to a text that traces the fleeting nature of human bliss without the usual finger-pointing. In fact, endowing dreams with the power to enlighten individuals is a fairly established trope in Chinese literature. This can be exemplified by Shen Jiji's narrative *Account of the World inside a Pillow* (枕中記 Chen zhong ji, 8th century), in which Lu Sheng, an unaccomplished scholar, borrows a pillow from a Daoist priest and takes a nap. In his dream, he crawls into the pillow and finds a kingdom where everything is laid out for him. In the following fifty years, he realizes all his goals for personal accomplishment. Suddenly, he wakes up only to find that his pot of millet is not yet fully cooked. Enlightened by this dream, he resolves to stifle his worldly desires. This tale reflects the Buddhist and Daoist outlook on life, which contends that human affairs are nothing but illusion.[26] Wise people save themselves endless worry and pain by abstaining from worldly ambitions. Despite the brevity of Zhang Sheng's dream, it shares with Lu Sheng's pillow story the soteriological purpose: the hero strives for a worldly good – that is, Yingying's love – which he seemingly achieves, but then he loses it and wakes up.

According to Jin's interpretation, the rest of the story can be read between the lines. This said, Jin also admitted that his interpretation takes liberties; after all, he breaks away from the conventions established by Mencius. The play's author, Wang Shifu, is no longer assigned the ultimate authority on the text's appearance. Jin justifies his radical rewriting of the drama with the following words: 'I cannot say whether my comments agree with the ideas of the author or not. If they do, regard this edition of *The Western Chamber* as the one which is for the first time understood. If not, consider *The Western Chamber* which is already known as one book, and consider this edition as another book altogether, being the ideas and thoughts of Shengtan [i.e. the author].'

Oneiric destabilization in *Dream of the Red Chamber*

Unsurprisingly given its title, Cao Xueqin's (1715/24–1763/64) novel *Dream of the Red Chamber* features a plethora of dreams which enter the sprawling narrative – David Hawkes's English translation runs to approximately 2500 pages – at various levels. As in *Plum in the Golden Vase*, some are embedded in the primary realist narrative, and as in *Peony Pavilion*, they also provide shortcuts to the metaphysical narrative which frames the realist plot. And similar to the reception history of *Western Chamber*, these dreams have been the object of many scholarly debates. *Dream of the Red Chamber* tells of the fortunes of the Jia clan, an aristocratic family, mainly through the eyes of Jia Baoyu, a princling who was born with a piece of jade in his mouth. Baoyu seems bound to disappoint the high hopes that are put on him as a future clan leader, as he shows a clear preference for the products of artistic refinement over aquiring the kind of erudition necessary for courtly recognition. Much of the plot revolves around the upsets and tiffs between Baoyu and his circle of friends, which are frequently embedded in poetry competitions (鬥詩 doushi) or written exchanges. The text abounds with Daoist and Buddhist references on multiple levels. This begins with a very superficial treatment of the *Zhuangzi*.

When Baoyu draws the ire of multiple girls at the same time, the angered youth retreats into his study to read in the *Zhuangzi* about the fleetingness of all earthly things. When his melodramatic mood increases, he grows convinced that he has attained Enlightenment, so he starts to write poetry that affects the sound of Daoist and Buddhist philosophy. Eventually, Baochai, his future fiancé, grows worried about his state of mind: 'Those Taoist writings and Zen paradoxes can so easily lead people astray if they do not understand them properly. I shall never forgive myself if he is going to start taking this sort of nonsense seriously and getting it fixed in his head' (DRC I, 441). As Baochai and Daiyu, his love interest, berate him for his ignorance concerning canonical writings of wisdom, he instantly lets down his guard, thinking: 'It was clear that their understanding of these matters was far in advance of his own. He consoled himself with the reflection that if they, whose understanding was so superior, were manifestly still so far from Enlightenment, it was obviously a waste of time for *him* to go on pursuing it' (443). In this scene, the unsettling power of Daoist writing is downplayed as inconsequential nonsense – only to prepare the reader for a cascade of metaphysical twists and turns.

One day, the rumour reaches Baoyu that a boy has shown up who carries the same first name. Irked by this possibility, he starts sulking and dreams of meeting him:

> Soon he had drifted into sleep.
>
> He was in a garden, which, he remarked with surprise, bore some resemblance to Prospect Garden [i.e. in the Jia clan's scenic landscape park]. While he was still puzzling over the similarity, he became aware that some girls were coming towards him, all of them maids. [...] Bao-yu [...] smiled back at them:
>
> 'I've strayed in here by accident. I think this garden must belong to some friend or other of my family. Won't you take me with you and show me round it?'
>
> 'It isn't our Bao-yu after all,' said the girls. 'He's not bad-looking, though, and he *sounds* reasonably intelligent.'
>
> 'Tell me,' said Bao-yu eagerly, 'is there another Bao-yu here then?'
>
> '*Bao-yu*?' rejoined one of the girls sharply. '*We* have Her Old Ladyship's and Her Ladyship's orders to use that name as much as possible as a means of bringing him luck and Bao-yu likes to hear us use it; but what business has a boy like you from some remote place outside to be making free with it? Don't let them catch you doing that here, *boy*, or they'll flay your backside for you!'
>
> 'Come, let's be going,' said another. 'We don't want Bao-yu to see him.'

'Don't let's stand here talking to the nasty creature,' said a third. 'We shall be contaminated!'

And they hurried off.

Bao-yu was nonplussed: 'No one has ever been as horrid as that to me before. I wonder why they are? And I wonder if there really *is* another person exactly like me here.'

As he mused on the unaccountable hostility of the maids, his feet were carrying him along in no particular direction and presently he found himself inside a courtyard. [...] He mounted the steps of the verandah and walked inside the building. Someone was lying there on a bed. On the other side of the room were some maids, some of them sewing, some of them giggling over a game they were playing. Presently the person on the bed – it was a youth – could be heard to sigh and one of the maids laughingly inquired what he was sighing for.

'Aren't you asleep, Bao-yu? I suppose you are worried about your cousin's illness again and imagining all sorts of foolish things about her.'

Bao-yu heard this with some astonishment. He listened while the youth on the bed replied:

'I heard Grandmother say that there is another Bao-yu in the capital who is exactly like me, but I didn't believe her. I've just been having a dream in which I went into a large garden and met some girls there who called me a 'nasty creature' and wouldn't have anything to do with me. I managed to find this Bao-yu's room, but he was asleep. What I saw was only an empty shell lying there on the bed. I was wondering where the real person could have got to.'

'I came *here* looking for Bao-yu. Are *you* Bao-yu then?' Bao-yu could not help blurting out.

The youth leaped down from the bed and seized Bao-yu by the hands:

'So *you* are Bao-yu, and this isn't a dream after all?'

'Of course it isn't a dream,' said Bao-yu. 'It couldn't be more real!'

Just then someone arrived with a summons:

'The Master wants to see Bao-yu.'

For a moment the two Bao-yus were stunned; and then one Bao-yu hurried off and the other Bao-yu was left calling after him:

'Come back, Bao-yu! Come back, Bao-yu!'

Aroma [his servant] heard him calling his own name in his sleep and shook him awake.

'Where's Bao-yu?' she asked him jokingly.

Though awake, Bao-yu had not yet regained consciousness of his surroundings. He pointed at the doorway:

'He's only just left. He can't have got very far.'

'You're still dreaming,' Aroma said, amused. 'Rub your eyes and have another look. That's the mirror. You're looking at your own reflection in the mirror.' (DRC III, 86–87)

Subsequently, some attendant recalls that Baoyu's grandmother had warned them not to set up too many mirrors around him:

> She says that when you're young your soul isn't fully formed yet, and if you're reflected in mirrors too often, it can give your soul a shock which causes you to have bad dreams. Fancy putting your bed right in front of that great mirror! It's all right as long as it's kept covered [...]. [Y]ou must have been looking at yourself in it before you dropped off to sleep. That would be a sure way of bringing on a bad dream. (87)

At the plot level, this 'rationalist' explanation, which accords with modern *fengshui* advice,[27] sufficiently explains Baoyu's spectacular dream, so that nobody gives this *mise-en-abyme* a second thought. On a wider scale, however, the dream is related to the metanarrative that frames Baoyu's biography. After all, the *doppelgänger*'s last name is Zhen Baoyu (甄寶玉 homonymous with 'the true Baoyu'), in contrast to the protagonist's own full name, Jia Baoyu (賈寶玉 homonymous with 'the false Baoyu'). By way of this word play, their encounter reimagines the *Zhuangzi*'s butterfly dream in a new setting: 'But he didn't know if he were Jia Baoyu who had dreamed he was Zhen Baoyu or Zhen Baoyu dreaming he was Jia Baoyu. Between Zhen Baoyu and Jia Baoyu, there must be some distinction!' What is more, by means of a word play, the dream emphasizes the Daoist dichotomy of 'falseness' (假 jia) and 'truth' (真 zhen) which runs through the entire text. According to Ying Wang, this polarity creates a narrative split into different realms, juxtaposing the protagonists' 'false' perspective on the world with the enlightened wisdom of the omniscient narrator who provides the reader with 'broader and wiser visions than those available to the mortal characters.'[28] It follows that the *mise-en-abyme* dream gives Baoyu a chance to internalize a statement that his *doppelgänger* articulates: 'What I saw was only an empty shell lying there on the bed.' Baoyu is an empty shell; after all, the Transformation of Things encourages humans to yield to incessant change. Consequently, this dream boils down to the lesson learned by Zhang Sheng in Jin Shengtan's interpretation of *Western Chamber*: it is not worth the trouble to attach oneself to this fleeting world.

Dream of the Red Chamber does not stop at inserting 'strange dreams' within an otherwise realist setting of the story, it also frames the main narrative with a karmic story of retribution. In contrast to common narratives, however, karmic debt is not accumulated in the human but in the spiritual realm. Initially this thread of causation is revealed to Zhen Shiyin, a minor character, by way of a dream. He learns that Crystal Page, a supernatural being, had regularly watered with dew Sylph Herb, an anthropomorphic plant, until it obtained its full human shape. On receiving this favour, Sylph Herb realized that it could not repay Crystal Page within the confines of the spiritual realm. Eventually both agreed on being reincarnated on earth to realize Sylph Herb's somewhat bizarre plan: 'The only way I could perhaps repay him would be with the tears shed during the whole of a mortal lifetime if he and I were ever to be reborn as humans in the world below' (DRC I, 53).

Subsequently they are reincarnated as Baoyu and Daiyu, the protagonists in the realist narrative. Throughout the book the relevance of this karmic bond is mentioned repeatedly, not only by the narrator and the Fairy in Baoyu's dream, but also by a Buddhist monk, who at one point openly addresses the boy's previous life: 'From drunken dreaming one day you'll recover: Then, when all debts are paid, the play will soon be over' (DRC I, 505). Akin to the *Zhuangzi*'s dream, the text exhibits a confusing notion of reality: two spiritual beings settle an old account by having two humans experience the vicissitudes of life. This meta-narrative voices a renunciatory attitude towards life by advancing a metaphysical vision that disregards the pathos of salvation. Since Daiyu's tears are mere substitutes for the water, which was used to nourish the spiritual plant, the concrete causes of her sorrows – the clan's ruthless utilitarianism – become secondary.

Understandably, readers reacted with disbelief at the causal connection between the two narratives: as Daiyu dies of consumption while Baoyu, who has lost his mind, is married off to her rival, one finds it difficult to regard Sylph Herb's debt of gratitude as a satisfactory answer to their failed love story.[29] In line with this reservation, Red Ink Studio (脂硯齋 Zhi yan zhai), an anonymous contemporary commentator of the 18th century, expresses surprise at the passage that relates the karmic bond: 'Reader, please put down the book here and think: have you ever come across such a passage in a book? I have never read anything as bizarre.'[30] The text, we learn, does not build on a common understanding, but stretches Daoist concepts to such an extent that even contemporaries found difficult to follow. Nonetheless, other early critics did look favourably on the moral function of the meta-narrative. Zhang Xinfa, for example, keenly defends the book's moral message but regrets that it remains hidden for most readers:

> The [*Dream of the Red Chamber*] is not only a book that appeals to people's taste. Its power to engrave itself on the hearts and alter the character of its readers make it a more potent malice than [*Plum in the Golden Vase*]. This is because readers see only the apparent side [正面 zhengmian] of the book and can't see its hidden side [反面 fanmian]. Now and again comes an observant reader who can tell the difference.[31]

Despite Zhang's generous assessment of the 'hidden side,' identified as the narrative voice that makes a case for renunciation, he still takes exception to the 'apparent side,' which follows the life story of the 'most lustful person' Baoyu. And indeed, even if one emphasizes the book's 'hidden side,' it is hopeless to isolate one single stratum of meaning. In this regard, Andrew H. Plaks argues:

> The possibility of interpreting the entire 'red-chamber dream' as a false illusion – the opposite of the 'true' vision of the Buddhist monk [and] the Taoist priest [...] – presents itself repeatedly in the course of the long novel. But it will be argued in conclusion that within the breadth of vision that characterizes the work as a whole, even truth and falsity, reality and illusion, must be treated as complementary possibilities rather than dialectical antitheses.[32]

Accordingly, the Daoist principle of bivalence is so deeply woven into the text that not even the escapist values which Jin Shengtan read into *Western Chamber* – that is, enlightenment through renunciation – have the final say.

In the wake of Chinese modernity, critics started concentrating on the text's realist narrative rather than on its spiritual message: the story of the Jia clan's downfall was increasingly regarded as the primary artistic feat of *Dream of the Red Chamber*. To facilitate the text's rediscovery as a proto-realist novel, critics like Hu Shi (1891–1962) downplayed the significance of the karmic metanarrative. But now the problem was that some aspects of the story no longer suited its presumed secular outline, in particular the novel's tragic end. Consequently, Hu asserted that the end – which was in fact written by another author – stood at odds with the novel's plan. In his eyes, the story does not answer to the metanarrative, as its characters deserve a happy ending: 'The great tragic end breaks with the belief in a happy end typical for Chinese *xiaoshuo*.'[33] Hu's advocacy for the text helped to elevate it to the status of a national treasure, thereby also laying the ground for its Maoist reappraisal. Stripped of its fantastic dimension, the text was even considered compatible with socialist realism.[34]

Conclusion

The interpretation of dreams carries the power to unsettle realities. In *Plum in the Golden Vase*, this is exemplified on a small scale: Wu Song has the suspicion confirmed that his elder brother was murdered. In *Peony Pavilion*, Liniang's erotic oneiric encounter with Liu Mengmei leads to her premature death and, in the long run, to the fulfilment of her romantic destiny. This reality-changing power is not limited to how dreams are negotiated within the narratives, but goes beyond the diegesis, as it also applies to the texts' critical interpretations. Jin Shengtan puts Zhang Sheng's dream at the heart of his understanding of *Western Chamber*, and in a similar manner, critics tried to promote their reading of *Dream of the Red Chamber* by emphasizing or downplaying the oneiric dimension. Rather than merely reiterating established concepts of oneirology, two of our four texts also challenge and expand them considerably. Liniang's iconoclastic dream endows the supernatural encounter previously reserved for sages and kings (Wu Ding's dream of Fu Yue) with an erotic dimension. And in shifting the focus away from the human realm, Sylph Herb's idea of repaying her debt of gratitude perverts the notion of the karmic circle.

Arguably, the central aesthetic tension in *Dream of the Red Chamber* lies in the clash between the text's mystical elements and the realist setting that dominates the narration. While the surprisingly integration of both factors may have contributed to the book's enduring resonance with audiences from the Qing period through to the present, critics of the early twentieth century were determined to carve a novel – the Western genre – out of this *xiaoshuo*. This came at the expense of the aspects that Red Ink Studio labelled 'bizarre,' including the dreamy metanarrative. As Hu Shi's critical work focused on the literary text as a testimony to the author's subjective experience and Mao Dun (1896–1981), a social-realist author, issued a purged version of the text that elided all metaphysical layers,[35] Baoyu's Zhuangzian dream vision about his *doppelgänger* also appears in a new light. From now on, the oneiric realm was supposedly rooted in the author's psychology and not in a transcendental supralayer that imposes itself on the sphere of mortals. Such radical reinterpretations and rewritings took issue with those mystical, often playful elements that had been integral to literary production in Chinese literary history from its inception in antiquity. The next chapter closes in on 'tales of the strange,' in which 'strange dreams' like Baoyu's play a central role.

Notes

1 The text evinces a complex editorial history. The two most influential versions are the *Red Ink Studio's Annotated Story of the Stone* (脂硯齋重評石頭記), an annotated copy written in 1759, and the Cheng-Gao editions (程高本) – that is, the full 120-chapter versions which appeared in 1791 and 1792.
2 Liu Degang, for example, once suggested that *Dream of the Red Chamber* should be viewed as the symptom of a teleological development of Chinese *xiaoshuo*, literary texts written in the vernacular, towards the Western novel. See Liu Degang (劉德剛), '*Dream of the Red Chamber* Read Overseas' (海外讀紅樓夢), *Hong Lou Meng xuekan* (紅樓夢學刊) 7.4 (1986), 87–106, here 101–103.
3 Andrew H. Plaks, *The Four Masterworks of the Ming Novel* (Princeton: Princeton University Press, 1987), 70.
4 Indented lines indicate the use of a proverb, use of Classical Chinese or a literary reference.
5 Lanling Xiaoxiao Sheng (蘭陵笑笑生), *The Plum in the Golden Vase or, Chin P'ing Mei*, trans. by David Tod Roy, 5 vols (Princeton: Princeton University Press, 1993–2011), I, 178–179. Henceforth quoted as PGV with numbers of volume and page.
6 See Mu-chuo Poo, 'The Concept of Ghost in Ancient Chinese Religion', in: *Religion and Chinese Society*, ed. by John Lagerwey, 2 vols (Hong Kong: Chinese University Press, 2004), I, 173–192, here 178.

7 See Jan Jakob Maria De Groot, *The Religious System of China: Its Ancient Forms, Evolution, History and Present Aspect, Manners, Customs and Social Institutions Connected Therewith*, 6 vols (Leiden: Brill, 1892–1910), IV (1901), 744.
8 The text started to circulate in two versions: a complete version reserved for secret libraries and a popular abridged version which circulated among the general public. See Naifei Ding, *Obscene Things: Sexual Politics in Jin Ping Mei* (Durham: Duke University Press, 2002), 33–35.
9 See Martin W. Huang, *Desire and Fictional Narrative in Late Imperial China* (Cambridge, MA: Harvard University Press, 2001), 142–144.
10 In Chapter 27, Ximen copulates with pregant Liping while Jinlian evesdrops on them. Immediately afterwards, Ximen and Jinlian proceed to engage in a lengthy orgy in the grape arbor which is described in great anatomical detail.
11 Orig. '手挽同心，舌分香唾，酒興浸透春心。金桂自覺難禁，解開底衣，和月白衣人兒在葡萄樹下，使一條白綾汗巾斜分其股，恣意取樂。月白衣人取將一件東西，紫團團有茄子大，徐徐用其唾，納入金桂牝中。爽美異常，不覺淫精四溢。只見月白衣人解開綾巾，扶她睡入帳中。那金桂昏迷不醒。忽然雞叫一聲，月白羅衣人不見。梅玉又來送回金桂門首，說：'姐姐將息幾日，我且不來了。' Ding Kangyao 丁耀亢, *Three Continuations of Plum in the Golden Vase* (金瓶梅續書三種), 2 vols (Ji'nan: Qilu chubanshe, 1988), II, 301. Henceforth quoted as XJP.
12 Orig. '今日又犯了葡萄架的淫根，故此鬼魅狐妖乘虛而入，化出當年西門慶的形象，攝其魂魄。不覺淫精四散，元氣大傷，白日胡言亂語，飲食不進，染成大病，一臥十日不起。' (XJP 303).
13 Tang Xianzu (湯顯祖), *The Peony Pavilion*, trans. by Cyril Birch (Bloomington: Indiana University Press, 1980), ix. Henceforth quoted as PP.
14 This poem is by no means renowned for its eroticism. No lesser authority than Confucius asserted: '*The Cry of the Osprey* expresses joy without becoming licentious, and expresses sorrow without falling into excessive pathos.' Confucius, *Analects: With Selections from Traditional Commentaries*, trans. by Edward Slingerland (Cambridge, MA: Hackett, 2003), 25. For further translations of the first lines of the Shijing, including one by Ezra Pound, see John Minford and Joseph S.M. Lau (eds.), *Classical Chinese Literature: An Anthology of Translations: From Antiquity to the Tang Dynasty* (New York: Columbia University Press, 2000), 75–77.
15 For a summary of Mencius' intentional theory, see Longxi Zhang, *The Tao and the Logos: Literary Hermeneutics, East and West* (Durham: Duke University Press, 1992), 134–135.
16 This approach was further elaborated by the Mao-Zheng tradition of interpreting poetry. According to this canonical commentary to the *Classic*

of Poetry, the *Maoshi Zhengyi* (毛詩正義), poetry is defined as 'where the intent goes: what is in the heart is intent; once manifested as words it becomes poetry.' Yu-yu Cheng, 'Text and Commentary in the Medieval Period', in: *The Oxford Handbook of Classical Chinese Literature (1000 BCE – 900 CE)*, ed. by Wiebke Denecke et al. (Oxford: Oxford University Press, 2017), 123–132, here 124.

17 The branch in Liu Mengmei's hand hints at his name, willow (柳 liu) being a homophone of his surname (劉 Liu).

18 The idiom derives from the *Rhapsody of Gaotang* (高唐賦 Gaotang fu), a poem dating from the 2nd century BC. It tells the story of the King of Chu, who ascends to Wu Mountain and makes love with a mysterious woman in a dream. On parting, the woman tells him: 'At dawn I am the morning cloud, at evening I am the driving rain.' Quoted in: Lynn Pan, *When True Love Came to China* (Hong Kong: Hong Kong University Press, 2015), 39.

19 See Paolo Santangelo, *Sentimental Education in Chinese History* (Leiden: Brill 2003), 303. This notion of love as a power that braves all adversities of life and even death – after all, Liu Mengmei emphasizes: 'I am dying of love (愛殺 ai sha) for you' – can be identified as a stable concept from the 6th century onwards.

20 Tina Lu, *Persons, Roles, and Minds: Identity in 'Peony Pavilion' and 'Peach Blossom Fan'* (Stanford: Stanford University Press, 2001), 23.

21 Shifu Wang, *The Story of the Western Wing*, trans. by Stephen H. West and Wilt L. Idema (Berkeley: California University Press, 1995), 219. Henceforth quoted as WW.

22 Folklore has it that pulling the sleeves tests whether someone is a ghost or not.

23 This mythological bird, *luan* (鸞) in the Chinese original, is related to the phoenix.

24 See Wen-Chin Hsu, '*The Romance of the Western Chamber*: Development in Literature and Its Reception in Society', *International Journal of Open University of Kaohsiung* 1 (2003), 133–153.

25 See Sally K. Church, 'Beyond the Words: Jin Shengtan's Perception of Hidden Meanings in *Xixiang ji*', *Harvard Journal of Asiatic Studies* 59 (1999), 5–77, here 47.

26 See Yuming Luo, *A Concise History of Chinese Literature*, trans. by Ye Yang, 2 vols (Leiden: Brill, 2011), I, 402.

27 See Peter So, *A Complete Guide to Feng Shui* (Hong Kong: Forms, 2012), 166.

28 Ying Wang, 'The Disappearance of the Simulated Oral Context and the Use of the Supernatural Realm in *Honglou meng*', *Chinese Literature: Essays, Articles, Reviews* 27 (2005), 137–150, here 143.

29 See Lucien Miller, *Masks of Fiction in Dream of the Red Chamber: Myth, Mimesis, and Persona* (Tuscon: Arizona University Press, 1975), 86.

30 Orig. '觀者至此請掩卷歷來小說可曾有此句千古未聞。' Cao Xueqin (曹雪芹), *Red Ink Studio's Annotated* Story of the Stone (脂硯齋重評石頭記 Zhi Yan Zhai chong ping Shi tou ji), ed. by Zhou Xuanlong 周絢隆 (Beijing: Renmin wenxue chubanshe, 2009), 18.
31 Quoted in: Haun Saussy, 'The Age of Attribution: Or, How the *Honglou meng* Finally Acquired an Author', *Chinese Literature: Essays, Articles, Reviews* 25 (2003), 119–132, here 123.
32 Andrew H. Plaks, *Archetype and Allegory in the 'Dream of the Red Chamber'* (Princeton: Princeton University Press, 1976), 222–223.
33 Orig. '大悲劇的結束打破了中國小說的團圓迷信。' Hu Shi (胡適), 'Textual Criticism of *Dream of the Red Chamber*' (紅樓夢考證 Hong lou meng kaozheng), in: *Works* (文存 Wen cun), 3 vols (Shanghai: Ya dong tu shu guan, 1921), I, 866–867.
34 See Johannes D. Kaminski, 'Toward a Maoist *Dream of the Red Chamber*: Or, How Baoyu and Daiyu Became Rebels Against Feudalism', *Journal of Chinese Humanities* 3 (2017), 177–202.
35 See Roy Bing Chan, *The Edge of Knowing: Dreams and Realism in Modern Chinese Literature* (Seattle: Washington University Press, 2017), 79.

Bibliography

Cao, Xueqin (曹雪芹). *Red Ink Studio's Annotated Story of the Stone* (脂硯齋重評石頭記 Zhi Yan Zhai chong ping Shi tou ji). Ed. by Zhou Xuanlong 周絢隆 (Beijing: Renmin wenxue chubanshe, 2009).
Chan, Roy Bing. *The Edge of Knowing: Dreams and Realism in Modern Chinese Literature* (Seattle: Washington University Press, 2017).
Cheng, Yu-yu. 'Text and Commentary in the Medieval Period', in: *The Oxford Handbook of Classical Chinese Literature (1000 BCE – 900 CE)*, ed. by Wiebke Denecke et al. (Oxford: Oxford University Press, 2017), 123–132.
Church, Sally K. 'Beyond the Words: Jin Shengtan's Perception of Hidden Meanings in Xixiang ji', *Harvard Journal of Asiatic Studies* 59 (1999), 5–77.
Confucius. *Analects: With Selections from Traditional Commentaries*, trans. by Edward Slingerland (Cambridge, MA: Hackett, 2003).
De Groot, Jan Jakob Maria. *The Religious System of China: Its Ancient Forms, Evolution, History and Present Aspect, Manners, Customs and Social Institutions Connected Therewith*, 6 vols (Leiden: Brill, 1892–1910).
Ding, Kangyao (丁耀亢). *Three Continuations of Plum in the Golden Vase* (金瓶梅續書三種), 2 vols (Ji'nan: Qilu chubanshe, 1988).
Ding, Naifei. *Obscene Things: Sexual Politics in* Jin Ping Mei (Durham: Duke University Press, 2002).
Hsu, Wen-Chin. 'The Romance of the Western Chamber: Development in Literature and Its Reception in Society', *International Journal of Open University of Kaohsiung* 1 (2003), 133–153.

Hu, Shi 胡適. *Works* (文存 Wen cun), 3 vols (Shanghai: Ya dong tu shu guan, 1921).

Huang, Martin W. 'Author(ity) and Reader in Traditional Chinese Xiaoshuo Commentary', *Chinese Literature: Essays, Articles, Reviews* 16 (1994), 41–67.

Huang, Martin W. *Desire and Fictional Narrative in Late Imperial* China (Cambridge, MA: Harvard University Press, 2001).

Lanling, Xiaoxiao Sheng (蘭陵笑笑生). *The Plum in the Golden Vase or, Chin P'ing Mei*, trans. by David Tod Roy, 5 vols (Princeton: Princeton University Press, 1993–2011).

Liu, Degang (劉德剛). 'Dream of the Red Chamber Read Overseas' (海外讀紅樓夢), *Hong lou meng xuekan* (紅樓夢學刊) 7.4 (1986), 87–106.

Lu, Tina. *Persons, Roles, and Minds: Identity in 'Peony Pavilion' and 'Peach Blossom Fan'* (Stanford: Stanford University Press, 2001).

Luo, Yuming. *A Concise History of Chinese Literature*, trans. by Ye Yang, 2 vols (Leiden: Brill, 2011).

Miller, Lucien. *Masks of Fiction in Dream of the Red Chamber: Myth, Mimesis, and Persona* (Tuscon: Arizona University Press, 1975).

Minford, John and Joseph S.M. Lau (eds.). *Classical Chinese Literature: An Anthology of Translations: From Antiquity to the Tang Dynasty* (New York: Columbia University Press, 2000).

Pan, Lynn. *When True Love Came to China* (Hong Kong: Hong Kong University Press, 2015).

Plaks, Andrew H. *Archetype and Allegory in the 'Dream of the Red Chamber'* (Princeton: Princeton University Press, 1976).

———. *The Four Masterworks of the Ming Novel* (Princeton: Princeton University Press, 1987).

Poo, Mu-chuo. 'The Concept of Ghost in Ancient Chinese Religion', in: *Religion and Chinese Society*, ed. by John Lagerwey, 2 vols (Hong Kong: Chinese University Press, 2004), I, 173–192.

Santangelo, Paolo. *Sentimental Education in Chinese History* (Leiden: Brill 2003).

Saussy, Haun. 'The Age of Attribution: Or, How the Honglou meng Finally Acquired an Author', *Chinese Literature: Essays, Articles, Reviews* 25 (2003), 119–132.

So, Peter. *A Complete Guide to Feng Shui* (Hong Kong: Forms, 2012).

Tang, Xianzu (湯顯祖). *The Peony Pavilion*, trans. by Cyril Birch (Bloomington: Indiana University Press, 1980).

Wang, Shifu (王實甫). *The Story of the Western Wing*, trans. by Stephen H. West and Wilt L. Idema (Berkeley: California University Press, 1995).

Wang, Ying. 'The Disappearance of the Simulated Oral Context and the Use of the Supernatural Realm in Honglou meng', *Chinese Literature: Essays, Articles, Reviews* 27 (2005), 137–150.

Zhang, Longxi. *The Tao and the Logos: Literary Hermeneutics, East and West* (Durham: Duke University Press, 1992).

3 Tales of the strange

Regardless of the prominence of dreams in Chinese literary history, one genre is particularly fond of challenging its protagonists' grasp of reality, so-called *zhiguai* (志怪) – that is, 'tales of the strange' or 'anomaly accounts.' Such narratives emerged during the late Han (2nd c. CE), flourished during the Tang (618–907), and remained relevant until the mid-Qing dynasty (18th c.). Here, dreams function as intermediate realms between the human and the supernatural spheres, allowing dreamers to make contact and engage in a dialogue with non-human agents. In some cases, they facilitate exciting one-night stands with shape-shifting foxes.

This chapter closes in on two short texts from ancient collections that can be considered as characteristic of the genre. Then, analyses of two further examples, Li Gongzuo's (778–848) tale 'Governor of Nanke' (南柯太守傳 Nanke tai shou zhuan, 8th c.) and Pu Songling's (1640–1715) *Strange Tales from a Chinese Studio* (聊齋志異 Liao zhai zhi yi, 1766), demonstrate the genre's flexibility with regard to soteriological messages and literary sophistication. Finally, the conclusion will address the theoretical problems posed by a genre that spans more than 2000 years.

Origins

Commonly assumed to be one of the first *zhiguai* collections, Liu Xiang's *Classic of Mountains and Seas* (山海經 Shan hai jing, 4th century BC) is exemplary in its generous inclusion of different kinds of knowledge. Its stories reference mythical creatures, such as Nüwa, the snake goddess, next to seemingly reliable pieces of information, such as the locations of riverheads. Altogether, the collection stands on the borderline of geography and fiction, which generates 'an appealingly imaginative space through which to journey.'[1] Other notable early collections include Gan Bao's *In Search of the Supernatural* (搜神記 Sou shen ji, 350 CE), Zhang Hua's *Treatise on Curiosities* (博物志 Bo wu zhi, 3rd c.), and Liu Jingshu's *Garden of the Extraordinary* (異苑 Yu yuan, 4th c.).

Arguably, the confusing epistemological position of such texts derives from their inclusion in the category *shi* (史), 'histories' – that is, narrations that subscribe to varying degrees of credence and reliability.[2] Rania Huntington finds that 'belief in some level of supernatural interaction with the human world was the mainstream view throughout the history of pre-modern China, but at the same time it was acknowledged that these were particularly fertile grounds for fabrication and delusion.'[3] This ambivalence fulfils an aesthetic and entertaining function from very early on; after all, the juxtaposition of bizarre content and its matter-of-fact presentation caters to the sensationalist, speculative predilections of its readers. While one can only make informed guesses about how such collections were read by their contemporaries, their classification as 'tales of the strange' was only established during the late Tang dynasty (618–907), denoting a particular type of supernatural historiography. Notably, its designated genre label, *zhiguai*, draws on a term first used in the *Zhuangzi*, the Daoist classic renowned for its fluid integration of reality and dream states.[4]

When later generations harked back to this designation, the term fulfilled a double function: while putting the truth of such narrations into question, its association with the *Zhuangzi* also pre-empted possible attempts to exclude them from the wider corpus of knowledge. This unzealous treatment contrasts with the waves of fanatical destruction of questionable knowledge, starting with the literary inquisition during the Qin dynasty (221–206 BC) through to the book burning under Emperor Qianlong (1735–1796). Instead, even disapproving censors put those texts aside as material deserving of future analysis. This lenient treatment facilitated their rediscovery by subsequent generations. Li Fang's *Extensive Records of the Taiping Era* (太平廣記 Tai ping guang ji, 978), for example, was prevented from circulation in print, as contemporaries branded the text as irrelevant for scholarly study. Thanks to the manuscript's well-preserved state, this vast collection was then rediscovered in the 16th century and revalued as one the greatest literary outputs of its time.[5] This changing assessment is emblematic for tales of the strange in general and highlights the genre's productive tension, drawing on both uncanonical sources of knowledge and aesthetic resourcefulness.

Dream accounts in classical 'stories of the strange'

Gan Bao's collection of strange tales, *In Search of the Supernatural*, dates from the Jin Dynasty (4th c. BC) and features an entire chapter devoted to dreams. The majority of them are prophetic in nature and directed at members of the imperial family. One of the most surprising dream accounts, however, is the story of a magical shirt given to a commoner:

> Liu Zhou, a clerk in the Selection Board during the Wu period, was seriously ill and had a dream that a person gave him a white Yuedan shirt. He said, 'Wear this garment, and when it is soiled, burn it and it will become clean.' When Zhuo awoke, there beside him was the shirt. Whenever it was soiled, he would always use fire to clean it.[6]

The function of the dream in this short text does not allow for any metaphysical speculations. Zhou falls ill and dreams of receiving a garment, then finds one upon waking up. There is a seamless integration of the extraordinary into the ordinary world, facilitated by the continued presence of a tangible object, the magical shirt. The unseen world, the reader is bound to believe, is a sphere that can pierce through the layers of our day-to-day reality at any time. Whether fancy items such as Zhou's shirt are meant simply to help mortals with the laundry or to cause metaphysical stupefaction is left unexplained – a typical feature of early *zhiguai* stories. Their authors refrain from commentary and proper narrative emplotment. In accordance with the story's straightforward outline, the narration is plain and sticks to non-metrical classical prose.

Quite in contrast to this first text, the majority of the dreams featured in *In Search of the Supernatural* focus on establishing the workings of fate. Such narratives usually follow a partition into two sections: the first gives the account of an enigmatic dream, the second of its conclusive interpretation on the part of a soothsayer or some authority. In this deictic cosmos, the dream of a splendid palace, for example, announces that the dreamer will assume the highest office in the administration one day. The vision of a black lizard foreshadows an illness. Since women do not qualify as objects of prophecy, their dreams' significance commonly relates to their husbands' and sons' lives only. An expectant mother, for example, has successive dreams of the moon and, later, of the sun entering her bosom. Her husband is delighted about these revelations, as he explains: 'The sun and the moon are the essences of *yin* and *yang* and are the most exalted of symbols. Our descendants are destined to flourish greatly!' (118). This said, context matters greatly for the correct interpretation of dream symbols, which change their meaning from case to case.[7]

For most of antiquity, such prophetic dreams were predominantly directed to members of the aristocracy. The *Extensive Records of the Taiping Era*, compiled around the end of the 10th century, extends this grace to scholars and imperial bureaucrats. In the following story, a poor mother learns of her child's future rise to glory:

> Xue Xia, born in Tianshui, was a very talented person and matchless in his learning. When his mother was pregnant with him, she dreamed that a caller came to her to present her with a box of clothing. He said: Madam, you will give birth to a wise and capable son, even the emperor will revere him. The mother took note of this dream and gave birth to Xia. When he was about twenty years of age, his learning was already remarkable. Day by day, Emperor Wen of Wei engaged in discussions with him. His diction was brilliant, his replies were smooth and never seemed dull. One day the emperor said: In the past, Gong Sunlong [a Chinese philosopher and writer, c. 325–250 BC] was called a great debater, but he was accused of being pedantic. But what you have said today is worthy of a saint's words. You are equal to Zi You and Zi Gong [two disciples of Confucius]. If the Great Sage were among us here in the state of Wei, he would find in you an accomplished man. Then the emperor handed a booklet to him, on which he had written the words: For a Learned Man. Xue Xia was then made secretary. Since he lived in a poor abode, the emperor took off his own clothes and passed them to him. This is all in line with his mother's dream. His name became famous and he established a line of eminent scholars.[8]

In this story, the dream-garment is not a magical item but indicates the future status of a yet unborn son. The dreamer does not require a diviner to interpret the dream but simply waits and observes the son's stellar career. While this type of dream reiterates the kind of prophecy first described in the *Classic of Poetry*, where a king dreams of bears and snakes, this report departs from the model in two ways: it features not only the rare appearance of a woman as the recipient of such dream, she also does not require help to interpret her vision. Apparently, dream language changed since ancient times, as prophecies adopt an increasingly straight-forward tone. The story's ideological message, however, remains the same: that fate is a decisive recruitment factor, and that the emperor can rely on the Mandate of Heaven to recruit the best people. In contrast to the chaotic, Daoist undertones in the story of Zhou's magical shirt, Xue Xia's dream is fully compatible with the beliefs of Confucian orthodoxy.

The soteriological dream in 'The Governor of Nanke'

The next text is also included in the *Extensive Records of the Taiping Era* and brings forward an entirely different form of dream. This one exemplifies the Buddhist notion of 'red dust' (紅塵 hongchen), the idea that the ultimate reality is concealed by the fog of material illusion. 'The Governor of Nanke' tells of an uneducated man who rises from rags to riches, only to discover that everything was a dream.[9] At the beginning of the story, Chunyu Fen looks back on a bumpy career. At one point in the past, he was appointed general of an army, but then indulged in excessive drinking until he was removed from office. Frustrated by this sacking, his unhealthy habit gets increasingly worse until he falls ill during a boozing session with friends who start to worry about him:

> 'You should get some sleep', they said to him. 'We'll feed the horses, wash our feet, and wait for you to recover before we go.' When Chunyu took off his headband and put his head on the pillow, everything went dark and seemed to spin about, as if in a dream.
>
> He saw two envoys clad in purple, kneeling before him, who said: 'The king of the Nation of Locust Tranquillity has sent us to deliver his message of invitation to you.' Chunyu got down off the couch unconsciously, straightening his clothing, and followed the two envoys toward the gate. There he saw a black-lacquered carriage driven by four steeds and seven or eight attendants. They helped him up into the carriage and departed, pointing to an

opening under the old locust tree as they went out the main gate. Then they sped into the opening. Chunyu found this most strange, but he didn't dare to ask any questions. Suddenly he saw that the landscape, climate, vegetation, and roadways were all markedly different from the world of men.[10]

Soon thereafter, the protagonist is summoned by the king:

> [T]he king said, 'Sometime before, I received your father's word that he wouldn't reject our small nation out of hand and he agreed to allow my second daughter, Jade Fragrance, to serve you respectfully as your wife.'
> Chunyu could only continue staring at the ground. He didn't dare to say anything.
> The king went on, 'Take him back to the guest lodge first, we will carry out the ceremony later!' [...] Chunyu thought this over. As far as he knew, his father had been a general on the border and because of that had fallen captive to the enemy, so that it wasn't known whether he was still alive. Had the king meant to say that after communicating with his father, who was among the northern barbarians, this matter had been concluded? His mind was very confused and he didn't really know how it had come about. (GN 519)

After an unsuccessful attempt to contact his father, Chunyu Fen finds the whole situation strange, without inquiring further into the matter though. Once he is introduced to the king's beautiful daughter, she immediately absorbs his fancy:

> She was about fourteen or fifteen and was just like an immortal. Preparations for the rites of the wedding night were also evident. From this time on, with each day Chunyu Fen's affection for her grew deeper as his star shone brighter at court. The carriages and vestments in which he went about, on excursions or at banquets, were always inferior only to those of the king. [...].
> After some time had passed, [the king] said to Fen, 'Our province of Southern Branch is not well governed. The governor has been dismissed and I'd like to engage your talents. If you would condescend to take such a limited position, you could go there with our young daughter!' Fen took these instructions to heart. The

king then ordered those in charge of such things to fit the new governor out for his journey. For this reason they arrayed gold and jade, brocades and silks, baskets and boxes, servants and maids, carriages and horses along a broad thoroughfare for the princess to take with her. [...] Twenty years after he took the position of governor, the people throughout the commandery had been reformed by his teachings and they all sang his praises. [...] The king greatly valued him and bestowed upon him further emoluments and land, also conferring on him rank and position, so that he became Prime Minister. (GN 521–524)

Similar to his former life, when Chunyu was suddenly removed from office, he once again runs out of luck. First, his commandery comes under attack and is defeated, then his wife, the princess, dies all of a sudden. As a result, the king becomes suspicious of his son-in-law and places him under house arrest. Finally, he explains to his son-in-law that he must go home:

'You have been separated from your family for a long time. You ought to go home to your village for a time and see your relatives. You can leave your children here. They will want for nothing. After three years we shall send them to you.'

'But this is my home', Fen replied. 'Where else would I go?'

The king laughed and said, 'You come from the world of men – your home is not here!'

Suddenly Fen grew groggy with sleep and his sight was hazy for a while until he became aware of his former life again. Then he wept and asked to return there. The king turned to his attendants indicating they should see him off. Bowing repeatedly, Fen left, and again saw the two purple-clad envoys from before following him. [...] Not long after, they emerged from a hole and he saw the lane through his village which had not changed from former days. Deeply moved, he could not hold back his tears. [...] The two envoys [...] called out his name in a loud voice a few times and Fen then came back to his senses as before. He saw one of the household servants sweeping the courtyard with a broom and one of his retainers sitting on a bench washing his feet. The setting sun had not yet sunk behind the western wall of his compound and the wine left in their goblets was still glistening by the eastern window. In the dream which flashed by him it was as if he had passed an entire lifetime. (GN 525–526)

After waking up, Chunyu's story is not yet concluded. Searching for the mysterious opening which led him to those foreign lands, he discovers a tiny hole underneath the locust tree in his garden. Here, he finds an anthill, which neatly mirrors the locations of his dream world, including the royal palace, the province of the Southern Branch, even his wife's tomb. Eventually, he draws a radical conclusion from his dream encounter: 'Feeling [...] the transience of the Southern Branch and understanding man's life was only a sudden moment, Fen then rested his mind in the gate of the Tao, giving up wine and women.'

Despite the fantastic elements of the story, the story's compiler, Li Gongzuo (c. 778–848), insists on the authenticity of the narrative. Indeed, he says he met Chunyu in person and can bear witness to the truthfulness of the events:

> I inquired about these events and visited the places involved so that we went over them a number of times. As the events were all verifiable, I recorded and edited them into this account as matter for those fond of such things. [...] I hope it will be a warning to those young men who wish to steal their way into an official position. (GN 528)

In comparison to the other texts, this dream narrative features well-developed characters, who are not only stunned by strange events but react to them in a plausible manner. The narrative dwells on quaint details, be it textiles or landscapes. Its marked difference to earlier examples of the genre led 20th-century scholars to distinguish between *zhiguai*- and *chuanqi*-stories (傳奇). In contrast to the former, the term *chuanqi* (translated as 'legends of the marvellous') indicates the literary quality of the texts, de-emphasizes questions about their authenticity, and represents a prototype of the *xiaoshuo* genre.[11] Although the narrator's insistence on the tale's veracity seems to contradict this verdict, his flawed reasoning – 'the story is true because I was told so' – reproduces a narrative convention more than anything else. While modern scholars put forward different sociopolitical interpretations of this tale,[12] it is difficult to ignore its escapist philosophy. The process of enlightenment is put into place by revealing to its good-for-nothing protagonist a dimension of the world normally invisible to us. The tiny world of insects is blown up to real-life proportions, thus creating the impression of a busy world that carries on its affairs in our very midst at all times – 'a world of which we are normally unaware, but by which we might be overwhelmed if we had the eyes to see it.'[13] This vision destabilizes the anthropocentric everyday perspective on the world, allowing the protagonist to reach the conclusion that human and animal life have one thing in common: both are unstable and fleeting. Human existence is just as meaningless as the life of an ant, which can be destroyed by an accidental footstep. The world at large is nothing but 'red dust,' as Buddhist frameworks say. But does it follow that Chunyu Fen, the protagonist, is healed from false worldly aspirations? 'The Governor of Nanke' lacks the promise of salvation, thereby inheriting the Daoist conviction that the cosmos is ultimately instable.

The narrative twist towards the end of the story departs from the conventions of earlier *zhiguai* stories. The aim is not mere documentation of a strange event, but to convince readers of the falsehood of their worldly lives. In this vein, the fantastic narrative 'reflects the Buddhist and Taoist outlook on life which advocates that the worldly honour and humiliation are nothing but illusion.'[14] Notably, the text frequently employs the term *wu* (悟), indicating more than just physiological awakening but an awakening to the truth.[15] Indeed, in the 9th century, the rejection of public service in favour of a life devoted to religion was already a well-established practice.[16] Stories such as 'The Governor of Nanke' were instrumental in popularizing the lives of hermits and were adapted into highly successful dramas, such as Tang Xianzu's (1550–1616) play *Dream of the Southern Branch* (南柯記 Nanke ji, 1600).

Aestheticism in *Strange Tales*

The fourth dream sample is taken from the *zhiguai* collection Chinese readers regard as the culmination of the genre, Pu Songling's *Strange Tales from a Chinese Studio*, dating from the early 18th century. These stories 'violate' the rules of the genre by means of their highly elaborate literary style. The collection's roughly 500 stories are artistically polished, show a strong preference for romantic emplotment, and indulge in intertextual references to the classics. In this collection, dreams can also facilitate insight into the workings of fate, but most of the time they relate spooky encounters with supernatural creatures.

In the story 'Fox Enchantment' (董生 Dong Sheng), a fox-spirit (狐狸精 hulijing) is the focus of interest. In Chinese mythology, they are embodiments of dark *yin* energy and are nourished on male *yang*.[17]

The trouble starts when two young married men, Daydreaming Dong and Thoughtful Wang, join a party, where they allow a physician, who is well-versed in fortune-telling, to read their pulse.

> 'I have read many pulses in my time', he pronounced. 'But you two gentlemen have the strangest and most contradictory configurations I have ever encountered. One of you shows Long Life, side by side with contraindications of Premature Demise; the other one shows Prosperity, but with contraindications of Poverty. Strange indeed! And quite beyond my competence, I fear.' [...]
>
> Daydreaming Dong returned home late that same night and was exceedingly surprised to find the door to his study standing ajar. He had drunk a great deal, and in his inebriated state he concluded that he must have forgotten to bolt the door earlier that evening. He had after all set off in rather a hurry. In he went and, without bothering to light the lamp, reached under the covers, to feel if there was any warmth left in the bed. His hand encountered the soft skin of a sleeping body, and he withdrew it in some trepidation. Hurriedly lighting the lamp, he beheld a young girl of extraordinary beauty lying there in his bed, and stood for a moment ecstatically contemplating her ethereal features. Then he began to caress her and fondle her body, allowing his hand to stray to her nether regions, where to his great alarm he encountered a long bushy tail. His attempt to effect a speedy escape was cut short by the girl, who was now wide awake and seized hold of him by the arm.
>
> 'Where are you going, sir?'
>
> Dong stood there trembling in fear. 'Madam Fairy', he pleaded with her, 'I beseech you, have mercy!'
>
> 'What have you seen to make you so afraid of me?' said the girl, with a smile.
>
> 'I don't fear your face...' Dong stammered. 'I fear your tail.'
>
> She laughed. 'What tail? You must have made some mistake.'[18]

(ST 143–145)

As he checks again, her tail has disappeared. Immediately they proceed to make love, and it is only later that she explains she is a girl from Dong's past. A month into their secret affair, his physiological condition deteriorates, and the worried doctor tells him to refrain by all means from further intercourse: 'You are clearly bewitched. My earlier prognosis of Premature Demise has been borne out. I fear there is no cure for you.'

Prepared to fend off Dong's weak attempts at self-preservation, the girl eventually uses dreams to continue cohabiting with him, a situation that compares to the sexual dream related in Ding Yaokang's *Continuation of Plum in the Golden Vase*:

> When he reached home, the girl greeted him with sweet smiles and wanted him in bed with her at once. He protested vehemently, 'Leave me alone! Can't you see I am at death's door?'
> He turned his back on her.
> 'Do you really think you can still live?' she cried bitterly, shame and anger mingling in her voice.
> That night, Daydreaming Dong took his medicine and slept alone, but the moment he closed his eyes in sleep, he dreamed he was making love to the girl again, and when he awoke he found that he had ejaculated in his bed. He grew more afraid than ever, and went to sleep with his wife, who lit a lamp and kept a close watch over him. Still the dreams continued, and yet every time he awoke the girl was nowhere to be seen. A few days later, he began to cough up large quantities of blood, and before long he was dead. (ST 146–147)

Now the story turns its attention to Thoughtful Wang:

> Now some while after this, Thoughtful Wang (the friend whose fortune had also been told on that fateful evening) was sitting in his own study one day, when a young girl entered unannounced. He was immediately taken with her beauty, and made love to her without further ado. He asked her who she was and where she was from.
> 'I am a neighbour of your friend Daydreaming Dong, who was also a dear friend of mine', she replied. 'Poor man! A fox cast a spell on him and he is with us no more! Foxes can cast powerful spells. Men of erudition in particular, such as you and your friend, should guard against them.'
> Wang was deeply moved by her words and loved her all the more. As the days went by, he too began to waste away and his reason started to wander. One night, in a dream, Daydreaming Dong came and spoke to him: 'Beware! Your lover is a fox. First she took my life, and now she wants yours. I have already laid charges against her before the courts of the Nether World, hoping to bring some

comfort to my wounded spirit. On the night of the seventh day, you must burn some incense outside your room. On no account must you forget these words!'

Wang awoke and marvelled at this strange dream. He decided to speak to the girl.

'I am seriously ill', he said, 'and it may soon be all up with me. It would be advisable for us never to make love again.'

'Do not worry', she replied. 'All is destiny. If you are destined for a long life, then no amount of love-making is going to kill you. And if you are destined to die, no amount of abstinence will save you.'

She sat by him and toyed with him, smiling so sweetly the while that Wang was unable to restrain himself and soon found himself in her arms again. Every time they made love, he was filled with remorse. But he was incapable of resisting her advances. (ST 147)

Eventually the mentioned day comes, so he lights incense and, luckily for him, it has the desired effect. The fox loses its powers, admits to having killed his friend, and transforms back into a real fox, only to die in front of Thoughtful Wang. Afterwards, the unmoved ex-lover proceeds to skin the fox, a tested method to avoid its resurrection. Eventually, the fox spirit visits Thoughtful Wang for the last time:

'I have been before the court of the Nether World', said the fox. 'Judgement was given against your friend Dong, whose death was reckoned to have been the consequence of his own lust. But I was still found guilty of enchantment. They took away my Golden Elixir, the fruit of all my years of toil. They have sent me back to be reborn. Where is my body?'

'My servants knew no better and skinned it.'

The fox was greatly distressed. 'It is true that I drove many men to their death. I deserved to die long ago. But nonetheless, what a heartless man you are!'

She took her leave, sadly, bitterly.

Wang all but died of his illness. But after six months he was restored to health. (ST 148–149)

As the fox's reference to the Golden Elixir (金丹 jindan) makes clear, it is proficient in the art of sexual alchemy, an esoteric practice especially popular during the Ming dynasty.[19] According to *Strange Tales*, this technique is not only accessible to humans, but also to ghosts and foxes who can nurture themselves on the energy of dreaming men. According to *The Classic of Su Nü* (素女經 Su nü jing; c. 982), a medical treatise, physiological and spiritual factors create a dangerous pathology behind dream sex:

> This occurs when *yin* and *yang* do not have an opportunity to interact, and one's desire becomes overwhelming. Then ghosts and demons assume human appearance and engage in intercourse with them. […] Those who indulge in this for a long time become deranged.[20]

In this tale, dreams follow two purposes. First, foxes use them as a means to sleep with male humans despite their firm resolution to abstain from further debauchery. Second, the ghost of Dong appears in dreams to warn Wang, reflecting the ancient belief that dead people linger around their former dwellings until their spirits find rest. This setting facilitates a narrative subversion of the human-centred focus of *zhiguai*, as the story's most intriguing character is not human. In fact, both male protagonists are characterized by aptronyms, that is, names which are particularly suited to their owners – a device that usually indicates lack of psychological depth. In contrast to their blatant lack of self-reflection, as evinced by Dong's gullibility and Wang's callous murder, the fox's relentless quest for immortality is endowed with tragic dignity. While Dong and Wang seem like mere lechers, who cannot reign in their basic desires, the fox pursues a higher goal. Ultimately, this imbalance unsettles the Heavenly Order, which posits that humans should rank higher than spirits and ghouls because of their ability to according to the moral law.

Granted that tales of *zhiguai* is a heterogeneous genre, *Strange Tales* tests the possibilities of such stories. The collection follows neither a documentary purpose like early collections nor brings forward a moral message akin to 'The Governor of Nanke.' The tantric fox, a creature which also rose to prominence in Japanese folk mythology (see Figure 3.1), lends itself to multiple interpretations. One can argue with Kang Xiaofei that the seductive fox is a euphemism for pleasure women.[21] One can also understand these tales as sublime attempts to elevate vulgar folktales to the literary tastes of a highbrow audience.[22]

Figure 3.1 Bakemono no e by an unknown master (detail). Coloured ink on paper, Edo period. Brigham Young University, Tom Perry Special Collections. Reproduced with kind permission.

Finally, one can also focus on the author's preference for creating salacious meaning and disregard his work as 'a collection best known [...] for bringing to life male scholars' wildest sexual fantasies'[23] – a surprising claim considering the collection's reserved eroticism, particularly when held against racy classics like *Plum in the Golden Vase* or even *Peony Pavilion*.

As a classical text, Pu Songling's *Strange Tales* can indeed cater to many audiences. Considered in the context of the *zhiguai* tradition, Pu's collection stands out for an irreverent attitude towards philosophical orthodoxy. Judith Zeitlin already stated that the collection treats the 'strange' as a 'purely fictional and ironic construct, one predicated on the author's and the reader's mutual suspension of disbelief.'[24] Arguably, Pu's scepticism goes even further, as his stories ironize not only the realm of spirits and ghouls, but also the metaphysical foundations of neo-Confucian orthodoxy. His treatment of the Classics borders on the heretic. On the one hand, this shows in the characters themselves. In 'Fox Enchantment,' for example, the animal spirit emerges as the personality who arouses most interest.

On the other hand, this subversive trajectory also shows in Pu's literary allusions, a dimension that is lost in translation but which accounts for the book's appeal among the literati class up until today. As any annotated copy of *Strange Tales* in Chinese would point out, the passage relating Dong's first encounter with the fox makes a cheeky reference to a Confucian classic, the *Commentary of Zuo* (左傳 Zuo zhuan) dating from the 4th century BCE. As the fox takes the shape of a naked lady and Dong starts to feel her up, one detail gives away her true nature: the tail between her legs. Dong withdraws promptly, and as she asks him what caused his consternation, he answers: 'I don't fear your face, [...] I fear your tail' (我不畏首而畏尾).[25] This wording alludes to a passage of the venerable commentary, in which a duke engages in a diplomatic exchange with neighboring warlords and explains: 'Fearing for its head and fearing for its tail, there is little of the body left not to fear for' (畏首畏尾，身其余幾). Although such meticulous references may sound pedantic to readers who cannot access the referenced cultural archive, one may take note of the annotations of an early commentator, who did not fail to take note of the allusion, then added: 'Good laugh!'[26]

Conclusion

In the Chinese literary tradition, dreams mark the edges of reality. Once you step beyond the waking world, you are not entering a subjective reverie, as the European Enlightenment has it, but an area governed by strange creatures that remain enmeshed in the social and cultural fabric of Chinese feudal society. In the best case, these strange creatures interact with humans on benevolent terms. They donate magical shirts or facilitate self-realization. In the worst case, these interactions throw individual dreamers into the chaotic world of spirits and leave them to die a mysterious death.

In the present chapter, our understanding of *zhiguai* stories is informed by genre notions which go back to late-Tang editors. While 20th-century scholars amended their assumptions and started to distinguish between simple *zhiguai* and the more elaborate *chuanqi*, this dichotomy does little to frame their puzzling content. In this context, E.D. Hirsch's sweeping assertion that 'every disagreement about an interpretation is usually a disagreement about genre'[27] misses the point entirely (unless one assumes that *zhiguai* is not a 'valid' label to start with). On a more productive note, one can understand this genre as a template for narratives which aim to challenge and defy categorical dichotomies, such as history vs. fiction and natural vs. supernatural. Consequently, modern readers encounter greater difficulties reading *zhiguai* than their contemporaries. If we proceed to attribute a liminal status to the genre, as Mingming Liu proposes,[28] we must keep in mind that such solutions are just a fix for a modern epistemological need. After all, we cannot help but differentiate between *argumentative* and merely *narrative* speech acts. Whereas the latter places a text in the sphere of entertainment, the former assigns it a place within historiography.[29] Defying such bivalent classifications, *zhiguai* are a reminder that the neat separation between the discrete realms of aesthetics and historiography is a fairly modern invention.

In the above dream stories, our world is under constant attack from the spiritual realm, which interferes with our daily routines by means of gifts, prophecies, lessons of enlightenment, and sneaky seductions. Their narrative brevity is crucial for the speculative mindset of the genre. The aim is to document the rupture between the two realms and not to make sense of it. As readers, amid the lack of a reliable narrator, we share the protagonists' wonder at an incomprehensible world. These stories hardly qualify as sources of instruction and future

Tales of the strange 59

reference: how could anyone distinguish between a noxious creature like the fox in *Fox Enchantment* and Jade Fragrance, the benevolent insect spirit in *The Governor of Nanke*? *Zhiguai* stories are reluctant to provide concluding answers.

The genre's episodic outline only exacerbates its anarchic quality. The editors exhibit a generous worldview, in which Chunyu Fen's spiritual enlightenment ('The Governor of Nanke') possesses the same dignity as Xue Xia's path to worldly fame (*Extensive Records of the Taiping Era*). Acting as testimonies to the epistemological indifference of their unfazed compilers, all these stories are not meant to add up to a stable worldview but nurture a suspicious und cautious attitude toward the unknown. Pu Songling's ironic *Strange Tales* transform the genre into a game between well-read writers and readers. For once, classic learning transforms from oppressive dogma into a source of sophisticated merriment.

Notes

1 Rania Huntington, 'The Supernatural', in: *The Columbia History of Chinese Literature*, ed. by Victor H. Mair (New York: Columbia University Press, 2012), 110–131, here 120.
2 See Sarah Allen, 'Narrative Genres', *The Oxford Handbook of Classical Chinese Literature*, ed. by Wiebke Denecke et al. (Oxford: Oxford University Press, 2017), 273–287, here 273.
3 Huntington, 'The Supernatural', 112.
4 The *Zhuangzi* identifies the undocumented book Qi Xie (齊諧) as the source of the fantastical creatures, gigantic fish and birds, mentioned in the Chapter 'Enjoyment in Untroubled Ease' (逍遙遊 Xiao yao you). This book is then described as a 'zhiguai,' a tale of the strange.
5 See Alexei Kamran Ditter, Jessey Choo, and Sarah M. Allen, 'Introduction', *Selections from Taiping Guangji*, ed. by A. K. D., J. C., and S. M. A. (Indianapolis: Hackett, 2017), 1–30, here 5.
6 Gan Bao (干寶), *In Search of the Supernatural: The Written Record*, trans. by Kenneth J. DeWoskin and James I. Crump, Jr. (Stanford: Stanford University Press, 1996), 120.
7 This is exemplified by the story 'Zhou Xuan' (周宣) in the *Extensive Records of the Taiping Era*. Here, the protagonist pretends to have repetitive dreams about a dog sitting on grass. Each time he consults the fortune-teller, he gets a different answer.
8 Orig. '薛夏，天水人也，博學絕倫。母孕夏之時，夢有人遺一篋衣，雲。夫人必生賢明之子，為帝王所宗。母記其夢之時。及生夏，年及弱冠，才術過人。魏文帝與之講論，彌日不息，辭華旨暢，應對

60 *Tales of the strange*

如流，無有凝滯。帝曰。昔公孫龍稱為辯捷，而迂誕誣妄，今子所說，非聖人言不談，則子遊、子貢之儔。不能過也。若仲尼在魏，覆為入室焉。帝手制書與夏。題雲入室生。位至秘書丞。居甚貧，帝解禦衣以賜之，以符先夢。名冠當時，為一代高士。' Wu Zengqi 吳增祺 (ed.), *Ancient Novels from Han, Wei and the Six Dynasties* (舊小說：漢魏六朝 Jiu xiaoshuo: Han, Wei, Liu chao) (Shanghai: Shangwu yinshu guan, 1957), 96.

9 Prior to the dream's incorporation into the *Extensive Records*, it must have first been circulated in manuscript form and was first collected by Chen Han 陳翰 in his *Collection of Strange Tales* (異聞集, c. 840). See William H. Nienhauser, *Tang Dynasty Tales: A Guided Reader* (Singapore: World Scientific Publishing, 2010), 167.

10 Li Gongzuo (李公佐), 'An Account of the Governor of the Southern Branch.' Trans. by William H. Nienhauser Jr, in: *The Shorter Columbia Anthology of Traditional Chinese Literature*, ed. by Victor H. Mair (New York: Columbia University Press, 2000), 517–528, here 518. Henceforth quoted as GN.

11 Lu Xun (魯迅) (1881–1936), one of the founding fathers of Chinese modern literature, derived the origin of literary *xiaoshuo*-writing from *chuanqi* (傳奇), thereby endowing Chinese literary history with a teleological thrust. Today this stance seems increasingly questionable; after all, it reduces such texts to their role as proto-*xiaoshuo* and blanks out their intermediate position between historical and fictional writing. See Xiaofei Tian, 'Collections', in: *The Oxford Handbook of Classical Chinese Literature*, ed. by Wiebke Denecke, Wai-Yee Li, and Xiaofei Tian (Oxford: Oxford University Press, 2017), 219–233, here 227.

12 Some readers took the story for a satire on the practice of marrying royal princesses to regional satraps. See Bian Xiaoxuan (卞孝萱), *Collection of Tang Literature, Historiography and Essays* (唐代文史論叢 Tangdai wenshi luncong) (Taiyuan: Shanxi Renmin 1986), 27–47. By a different token, it was also understood as discussing the reconciliation between a dead father and a living son. See Carrie Reed, 'Messages from the Dead', *Chinese Literature, Essays, Articles, Reviews* (*CLEAR*) 31 (2009), 121–130.

13 Robert Ford Campany, *Strange Writing: Anomaly Accounts in Early Medieval China* (Albany: State University of New York Press, 1996), 355.

14 Luo Yuming, *A Concise History of Chinese Literature*, trans. by Ye Yang, 2 vols. (Leiden: Brill, 2011), I, 402.

15 As the king sends Chunyu back, he becomes 'aware of his former life' (晉然久之，方乃發悟前事), then finally 'understands man's life was only a sudden moment' (悟人世之倏忽). Li Gongzuo 李公佐, 'An Account of the Governor of the Southern Branch / 南柯太守傳' (bilingual edition), in: *Anthology of Tang and Song Tales: The Tang Song chuanqi ji of Lu*

Xun, ed. by Victor Mair and Zhenjun Zhang (Singapore: World Scientific Publishing Company, 2020), 164–193, here 192.
16 See Alan Berkowitz, 'Social and Cultural Dimensions of Reclusion in Early Medieval China', in: *Philosophy and Religion in Early Medieval China*, ed. by Lo Yuet Keung and Alan Kam-leung Chan (New York: State University of New York Press, 2010), 291–318, here 299.
17 Foxes' parasitic interaction with humans allows them to live hundreds of years. Xiaofei Kang explains: 'In the Chinese yin/yang dichotomy, yin is interpreted as negative, ghostly, evil, female, and impure, whereas yang is positive, celestial, virtuous, male, and pure. [...] Using the art of metamorphosis and magic, the fox often engaged in spiritual possessions of people.' See Kang Xiaofei, *The Cult of the Fox: Power, Gender, and Popular Religion in Late Imperial and Modern China* (New York: Columbia University Press, 2005), 18.
18 Pu Songling, 'Fox Enchantment', in: *Strange Tales from a Chinese Studio*, trans. by John Minford (London: Penguin, 2006), 143–149, here 143–145. Henceforth quoted as ST. Translation with slight amendments by the author.
19 Richard G. Wang, 'Review of Xiaofei Kang: *The Cult of the Fox*', *Monumenta Serica* 54 (2006), 533–536, here 535.
20 Cited in: Douglas Wile (ed.), *Art of the Bedchamber: The Chinese Sexual Yoga Classics* (New York: State University of New York Press, 1992), 93.
21 See Kang, *The Cult of the Fox*, 57.
22 See Chen Yun (陳贇), 'Concerns about Literary Style and Experimentation in Ming-Qing Dynasty *Xiaoshuo*' (明清文言小說的文體焦慮與尊體實驗), *Ming Qing Xiaoshuo Yanjiu* (明清小說研究) 3 (2014), 81–92, here 91–92.
23 See Tze-lan D. Sang, *The Emerging Lesbian: Female Same-Sex Desire in Modern China* (Chicago: Chicago University Press, 2003), 67.
24 Judith T. Zeitlin, *Historian of the Strange: Pu Songling and the Chinese Classical Tale* (Stanford: Stanford University Press, 1993), 41.
25 Pu Songling (蒲松齡), *Tales of the Strange* (聊齋志異 Liao zhao zhi yi), 3 vols, ed. by Zhang Youguan 張友鶴 (Shanghai: Zhonghua shuju, 1963), I, 134.
26 Orig. '一笑。' Pu, *Tales of the Strange*, I, 134.
27 Eric D. Hirsch, *Validity in Interpretation* (New Haven: Yale University Press, 1967), 98.
28 See Mingming Liu, *Theory of the Strange: Towards the Establishment of 'Zhiguai' as a Genre*, DPhil thesis University of California Riverside 2015, Website: https://escholarship.org/uc/item/3579w43t (last accessed 4 August 2023).

29 According to Monika Fludernik, every genre contains utterances which correspond to five different 'macrogenres': narrative, argumentative, instructive, conversational, and reflective. See Monika Fludernik, 'Genres, Text Types, or Discourse Modes? Narrative Modalities and Generic Categorization', *Style* 34 (2000), 274–292, here 282.

Bibliography

Allen, Sarah. 'Narrative Genres', in: *The Oxford Handbook of Classical Chinese Literature*, ed. by Wiebke Denecke et al. (Oxford: Oxford University Press, 2017), 273–287.

Berkowitz, Alan. 'Social and Cultural Dimensions of Reclusion in Early Medieval China', in: *Philosophy and Religion in Early Medieval China*, ed. by Lo Yuet Keung and Alan Kam-leung Chan (New York: State University of New York Press, 2010), 291–318.

Bian, Xiaoxuan (卞孝萱). *Collection of Tang Literature, Historiography and Essays* (唐代文史論叢 Tangdai wenshi luncong) (Taiyuan: Shanxi Renmin 1986).

Campany, Robert Ford. *Strange Writing: Anomaly Accounts in Early Medieval China* (Albany: State University of New York Press, 1996).

Chen, Yun (陳贇). 'Concerns about Literary Style and Experimentation in Ming-Qing Dynasty *Xiaoshuo*' (明清文言小說的文體焦慮與尊體實驗), *Ming Qing Xiaoshuo Yanjiu* (明清小說研究) 3 (2014), 81–92.

Ditter, Alexei Kamran, Jessey Choo, and Sarah M. Allen (eds.). *Selections from Taiping Guangji* (Indianapolis: Hackett, 2017).

Fludernik, Monika. 'Genres, Text Types, or Discourse Modes? Narrative Modalities and Generic Categorization', *Style* 34 (2000), 274–292.

Gan, Bao (干寶). *In Search of the Supernatural: The Written Record*, trans. by Kenneth J. DeWoskin and James I. Crump, Jr. (Stanford: Stanford University Press, 1996).

Hirsch, Eric D. *Validity in Interpretation* (New Haven: Yale University Press, 1967).

Huntington, Rania. 'The Supernatural', in: *The Columbia History of Chinese Literature*, ed. by Victor H. Mair (New York: Columbia University Press, 2012), 110–131.

Kang, Xiaofei. *The Cult of the Fox: Power, Gender, and Popular Religion in Late Imperial and Modern China* (New York: Columbia University Press, 2005).

Li, Gongzuo (李公佐). 'An Account of the Governor of the Southern Branch.' Trans. by William H. Nienhauser Jr, in: *The Shorter Columbia Anthology of Traditional Chinese Literature*, ed. by Victor H. Mair (New York: Columbia University Press, 2000), 517–528.

——. 'An Account of the Governor of the Southern Branch / 南柯太守傳' (bilingual edition), in: *Anthology of Tang and Song Tales: The Tang Song chuanqi ji of Lu Xun*, ed. by Victor Mair and Zhenjun Zhang (Singapore: World Scientific Publishing Company, 2020), 164–193.

Liu, Mingming. *Theory of the Strange: Towards the Establishment of 'Zhiguai' as a Genre*, DPhil thesis University of California Riverside 2015, Website: https://escholarship.org/uc/item/3579w43t (last accessed 4 August 2023)

Luo, Yuming. *A Concise History of Chinese Literature*, trans. by Ye Yang, 2 vols. (Leiden: Brill, 2011).

Nienhauser, William H. *Tang Dynasty Tales: A Guided Reader* (Singapore: World Scientific Publishing, 2010).

Pu, Songling (蒲松齡). 'Fox Enchantment', in: *Strange Tales from a Chinese Studio*, trans. by John Minford (London: Penguin, 2006), 143–149.

——. *Tales of the Strange* (聊齋志異 Liao zhao zhi yi), 3 vols, ed. by Zhang Youguan (張友鶴) (Shanghai: Zhonghua shuju, 1963).

Reed, Carrie. 'Messages from the Dead', *Chinese Literature, Essays, Articles, Reviews (CLEAR)* 31 (2009), 121–130.

Sang, Tze-lan D. *The Emerging Lesbian: Female Same-Sex Desire in Modern China* (Chicago: Chicago University Press, 2003).

Tian, Xiaofei. 'Collections', in: *The Oxford Handbook of Classical Chinese Literature*, ed. by Wiebke Denecke, Wai-Yee Li, and Xiaofei Tang (Oxford: Oxford University Press, 2017), 219–233.

Wang, Richard G. 'Review of Xiaofei Kang: *The Cult of the Fox*', *Monumenta Serica* 54 (2006), 533–536.

Wile, Douglas (ed.). *Art of the Bedchamber: The Chinese Sexual Yoga Classics* (New York: State University of New York Press, 1992).

Wu, Zengqi (吳增祺) (ed.). *Ancient Novels from Han, Wei and the Six Dynasties* (舊小說：漢魏六朝 Jiu xiaoshuo: Han, Wei, Liu chao) (Shanghai: Shangwu yinshu guan, 1957).

Zeitlin, Judith T. *Historian of the Strange: Pu Songling and the Chinese Classical Tale* (Stanford: Stanford University Press, 1993).

4 Erotic dreams

In Chinese cultural history, sexual dreams do not participate in the problematic trias of eroticism, pornography, and obscenity that can be observed in the Judeo-Christian tradition. In general, Chinese antiquity was comparably open to the non-reproductive benefits of cohabitation, as it was said to facilitate the balance of *yin* and *yang* forces in one's body. Indeed, regular sexual activity was seen as a health benefit. Precisely this stance also motivated a prohibitive assessment of wet dreams as an unhealthy drain of energy. With the import of occidental concepts to China, sexual dreams underwent a semantic shift, yet never lost their ability to connect individual and collective life.

This chapter discusses premodern vernacular fiction and modern prose in conjunction. The four case examples stretch across three centuries, from the early Qing into the Republican era (1912–1949), thereby covering one of the most drastic ruptures in Chinese history: the advent of occidental modernity. In the first two texts, dreams are still infused with supernatural meaning, as is typical for premodern oneiric concepts. In both Li Yu's *Carnal Prayer Mat* (肉蒲團 Rou pu tuan, 1693) and Cao Xueqin's *Dream of the Red Chamber*, sexual dreams function as tools that connect the spiritual and corporeal realms. Dream sex is not sinful but a phenomenon linked to medical conditions and karmic entanglement. This changed after the import of European concepts, notably the selective appropriation of modern psychology. How do modern literary dreams negotiate the transition from the classical paradigm to a primarily psychological approach? In three representative novellas – Yu Dafu's novellas *Moving South* (南遷 Nan qian, 1921), *Boundless Night* (茫茫夜 Mangmang ye, 1922), and

DOI: 10.4324/9781003481881-4

Guo Moruo's *Caramel Girl* (卡爾美夢姑娘 Ka'ermeimeng gu'niang, 1924) – sexual dreams incorporate Freudian ideas into oneiric prose. As individual dream spheres connect to the great dilemma of the Chinese nation at the onset of the 20th century, this incurs unexpected results.

Self-castration in *Carnal Prayer Mat*

Dating from the early Qing era, Li Yu's (1610–1680) *Carnal Prayer Mat*, a text written in 1657 and published in 1693, heavily draws on Buddhist themes. The narrative follows the frame narrative of renunciation, one may think of 'The Governor of Nanke,' while at the same time evincing a degree of sexual explicitness that is only second to *Plum in the Golden Vase*. Inevitably, this creates an uneasy tension between the two poles of asceticism and eroticism.

At the beginning, Weiyang Sheng, an excitable youngster, visits a sage who quickly diagnoses a mismatch between the latter's mental gifts and his striking appearance. He wonders:

> What a fine intelligence the man has! But the Creator is at fault for giving him this physical form. Why match a heart that was meant for the study of Buddha with a face that will lead to damnable deeds? In his looks and demeanour I see all the signs of a notorious satyr who [...] will wreak havoc in the women's quarters with his clandestine amours.[1]

The sage's premonition is accurate. Weiyang Sheng inaugurates his erotic tour de force by marrying beautiful Yuxiang, whom he soon abandons because she cannot satisfy his appetite. After undergoing genital surgery, supervised by Daoist medics, he finds himself equipped with enough sexual prowess to leave the most experienced female lovers awestruck. His stellar career as man of pleasure, however, comes to an abrupt end when he visits a famous courtesan in Beijing – who turns out to be his abandoned wife. Shamed by being found out, she commits suicide. Now he understands the workings of karma: 'while I took a man's wife and made her my concubine, someone took my wife and turned her into a prostitute' (CPM 222). Three years after his departure, he is ready to rejoin the monastery, where a final challenge waits.

The reformed man strives to become a saint. He engages in Zen meditation and devotes his days to perfecting his knowledge of

Buddhist teachings: 'Lest a life of luxury stimulate his lust again, he neither dressed nor ate well, but preferred to develop his religious vocation by exposing himself to hunger and cold' (CPM 227). The narrator points out that Weiyang Sheng's standards of sainthood are higher than those of his peers, notably in view of his sexual drive:

> Any young man joining the order has certain problems he must face. However strongly he tries to rein in his lusts, however firmly he tries to extinguish his desires, prayer and scripture reading will get him through the day well enough, but in the wee hours of the morning that erect member of his will start bothering him of its own according, making a nuisance of itself under the bedclothes, uncontrollable, irrepressible. His only solution is to find some form of appeasement, either by using his fingers for emergency relief or by discovering some young novice with whom to mediate a solution. (CPM 227)

Weiyang Sheng rejects such mitigation measures with the argument that masturbation leads to intercourse, and that homosexual practices, seen as a lesser evil, also lower the threshold for heterosexual encounters. His zealous commitment to ascetic life, however, creates a different hazard — that is, erotic dreams. In sleep, his mind reiterates his past experiences of sexual excess and debauchery (see Figure 4.1):

> One night he dreamed that some women came to worship at the temple. On approaching them, he was astonished to find that they were all old friends of his. Flora was there, as were Cloud and her sisters, and also his two eloping wives, Jade Scent and Fragrance.
> The sight of his wives infuriated [Weiyang Sheng], and he called on Flora and her nieces to help him catch them. But in the twinkling of an eye the wives vanished, leaving only the four friends, who drew him into a priest's cell and proceeded to do with him what they had done so often before. They undressed and were about to begin another contest, with [Weiyang Sheng]'s penis fitted into someone's vagina and ready in thrust, when all of a sudden he was awakened by a dog barking in a nearby wood and realized that he had been dreaming. That erect member of his, however, still assumed there was a treat in store for it, and it butted and burrowed here and there among the bedclothes looking for its old haunts.

Erotic dreams 67

Figure 4.1 Weiyang Sheng's Meditation Interrupted by Erotic Dreams by an unknown master (detail). Woodcut print on paper, Qing period. In: Li Yü, *Jou Pu Tuan: Ein erotisch-moralischer Roman aus der Ming-Zeit* (Braunschweig: Die Waage, 1965), 543. Image from the author's own copy.

[He] took it in his hand and was thinking of some way to appease it, when suddenly he stopped.

This is the root cause of all my sins, my nemesis, he thought. I don't have to take revenge on it, but I must not let it loose.

Having come to this conclusion, he banished the foolish idea from his mind and tried to get some sleep before it was time to get up and chant sutras again.

But he tossed and turned in bed and could not get back to sleep, tormented beyond endurance by the root evil under his bedclothes. So long as this accursed thing is attached to me, he thought, I'll always be bothered by it. The best solution is to cut it off and eliminate all the trouble it's going to cause me. [...] If I don't cut it off, I can never be anything more than an animal. Even if I cultivate my behaviour to perfection, the best I can hope for is to be reborn as a human being. How can I ever become a buddha?

Having arrived at this conclusion, he could not wait for daybreak. He lit the lamp, picked up a thin vegetable knife, and honed it a few times on the ewer. Then, taking his penis in one hand, be brought the knife down on it with all the force he could muster, slicing the organ right off.

Evidently he was destined to shed his animal fate and to be transformed, for the amputation did not feel terribly painful. From that time on, his desires ceased and his moral purpose gained in strength, and the perceptiveness shown in his religious studies grew steadily. (CPM 227–228)

Weiyang Sheng's painful experiences in the dust-stained, mortal world did not put an end to his physical desires; instead, he appears to have been as incurably chained to the sensual realm as ever. It turns out that his vow to observe chastity is constantly undermined by the body's routines. Having previously enhanced his sexual prowess by a drastic Daoist surgery, he happily embraces an equally radical method to rid himself of his exterior organ.

While the narration sheds no doubt on the success of this approach, placing the text's ethical standpoint is more complex. Most commentators have cast doubt on the text's spiritual ambitions, instead dubbing it a pornographic satire that makes ironic use of the renunciation trope. Patrick Henan, for example, argues for an intertextual reading: 'The retribution plot fascinated the Chinese novelist, and one can see why; it allowed him to work human experience into newer and more meaningful shapes. He did not need to believe in the actual possibility of metaphysical retribution, for both he and his readers accepted it as part of the machinery of causation in fiction.'[2] Wai-Yee Li also plays down the significance of retribution and renunciation. According to her, the basic plot should be read as an 'intermittently earnest defence of the role of sexual desire in human existence.'[3] This assessment pays respect to the sensual playfulness of the text but does not take into account the primacy of the Doctrine of the Mean (中庸之道 zhong yong zhi dao). According to the Confucian ethics of moderation, a wise man should avoid extreme behaviour, in the sensual realm as well as in view of ascetic fanaticism. From this perspective, Weiyang Sheng's mission is not the pursuit of sexual liberation but the taming of his propensity for excess, a challenge that he fails to master in both roles: as the rake Weiyangsheng and as the monk going by the name of Stubborn Stone (頑石 Wan Shi).

In the preface, the author addresses the conflict between the sages who promote chastity and, on the other hand, laymen who view sexual congress as fundamental for physiological health. Li Yu endorses the latter, arguing that regular, though not excessive, intercourse allows partners to balance the five elements in their bodies:

> Long-term use results in the mutual reinforcement of *yin* and *yang*, whereas excessive use brings the water and fire elements into conflict. When treated as medicine, sex relieves us from pent-up emotion, but when treated as food it gravely depletes our semen and blood. (CPM 2)

He illustrates the hazards of abstinence with the imperial court's eunuchs, who, unable to engage in sexual intercourse, age prematurely: 'Why, then, do they have even more wrinkles than anybody else? And why does their hair go white even sooner?' (CPM 1).

At the other end of the *zhongyong* scale lies uninhibited sexual debauchery. In the novel, such behaviour is not only demonstrated by Weiyang Sheng prior to his reformation, but also in the biography of Xuan Xuanzi, a cuckolded husband. When Weiyang Sheng engages in a passionate affair with the latter's beautiful wife, he is puzzled by her husband's lack of interest in her. She answers: 'In his youth he was a rake who had one affair after another. Day and night he'd be off wenching. He wasted his powers so badly that now, in middle age, he's quite useless' (CPM 140). Probably the same would have happened to Weiyang Sheng, had he not quit his hypersexual life after only three years. Now the converted man risks another extreme. After severing his organ, he becomes similar to the eunuchs.

Weiyang Sheng's career oscillates between the two extremes and fails to establish *zhongyong*. Quite possibly, the book's greatest virtue lies in its rejection of a final answer to the problem of human sexuality. With its committed attention to the benefits of non-reproductive sex, *Carnal Prayer Mat* prefigures an observation that Susan Sontag made in view of the Marquis de Sade's pornographic works: 'There is, demonstrably, something incorrectly designed and potentially disorienting in the human sexual capacity.'[4] As Li Yu demonstrates, this observation is applicable to different cultures across time, even if their proposed solutions differ considerably.

Nightly emissions in *Dream of the Red Chamber*

Similar to *Carnal Prayer Mat*, an uneasy tension between spirituality and eroticism also features prominently in Cao Xueqin's novel *Dream of the Red Chamber*. In one of the arguably most convoluted dreams in Chinese literary history, Chapter 5 is comprised of a multi-layered dream that starts as a supernatural vision replete with prophetic symbols and poetry, then gives way to a tangible sexual experience. The recipient of this dream vision is Jia Baoyu, then still a child who falls asleep in the luxurious bedchamber of Qinshi, a close female relative.

In the dreamscape, an elegant lady – who goes by the ominous name Fairy of Disenchantment (警幻仙姑 jinghuan xiangu) – guides Baoyu through twelve tableaus comprised of cryptic emblems and poems. They give a veiled preview of the abuse, violence, and abandon that central female characters will meet in the course of the novel but are lost on the young boy who shows little interest in decoding long-winded metaphors. Realizing that she cannot save him from experiencing human disenchantment in the flesh, the fairy reproaches him: 'Silly boy! You still don't understand (悟 wu), do you?' (DRC I, 84), using a term typically found in the context of spiritual enlightenment. In fact, the spiritual purpose of the dream was originally devised by Baoyu's ancestors, who are worried that their clan lacks a son who could restore the family's status, reputation, and wealth. They asked the fairy a favour:

Could you perhaps initiate [Baoyu] in the pleasures of the flesh
[...] to shock the silliness out of him? In that way he might stand
a chance to escape some of the traps that people fall into and be
able to devote himself single-mindedly to the serious things of
life. (137)

The surprising aim of his initiation is to calibrate his state of mind in
a way that prepares their descendent to pursue a career in the imperial
administration, a requirement that draws on the *Liezi*'s story of how
the Yellow Emperor acquired spiritual enlightenment before becoming
a wise ruler. That such ideals should also be observed by the adminis-
trative elite, however, brings an awkward undertone to the ancestors'
plan. In light of this conceptual confusion, the proposed strategy, to
immerse Baoyu in the pleasures of flesh, is fittingly paradoxical and
only has an adverse effect, at least in the short term. In answer to the
request made by Baoyu's ancestors, the fairy introduces him to her
little sister, Keqing, to engage in sexual intercourse. She explains:

'The time is propitious. You may consummate the marriage this
very night. My motive in arranging this is to help you grasp the fact
that, since even in these immortal precincts love is an illusion, the
love of your dust-stained, mortal world must be doubly an illusion.
It is my earnest hope that, knowing this, you will henceforth be
able to shake yourself free of its entanglements and change your
previous way of thinking, devoting your mind seriously to the
teachings of Confucius and Mencius and your person wholeheart-
edly to the betterment of society.'
    Disenchantment then proceeded to give him secret instructions
in 'the thing with clouds and rain' [i.e. the art of love]; then,
pushing him gently inside the room, she closed the door after him
and went away.
    Dazed and confused, Bao-yu nevertheless proceeded to follow
out the instructions that Disenchantment had given him, which led
him by predictable stages to that act which boys and girls perform
together – and which it is not my intention to give a full account
of here.
    Next morning he lay for a long time locked in blissful tenderness
with Ke-qing, murmuring sweet endearments in her ear and unable
to tear himself away from her. Eventually they emerged from the
bedroom hand in hand to walk together out-of-doors.

> Their walk seemed to take them quite suddenly to a place where only thorn-trees grew and wolves and tigers prowled around in pairs. Ahead of them the road ended at the edge of a dark ravine. No bridge connected it with the other side. As they hesitated, wondering what to do, they suddenly became aware that Disenchantment was running up behind them.
> 'Stop! Stop!' she was shouting. 'Turn back at once! Turn back!'
> Bao-yu stood still in alarm and asked her what place this was.
> 'This is the Ford of Error,' said Disenchantment. 'It is ten thousand fathoms deep and extends hundreds of miles in either direction. [...] If you had gone on walking just now and had fallen in, all the good advice I was at such pains to give you would have been wasted!'
> Even as she spoke there was a rumbling like thunder from inside the abyss and a multitude of demons and water monsters reached up and clutched at Bao-yu to drag him down into its depths. In his terror the sweat broke out over his body like rain and a great cry burst from his lips,
> 'Ke-qing! Save me!'
> Aroma and his other maids rushed upstairs in alarm and clung to him.
> 'Don't be frightened, Bao-yu! We are here!'
> But Qin-shi [...] marvelled to hear him call her name out in his sleep.
> '*Ke-qing* was the name they called me back at home when I was a little girl. Nobody here knows it. I wonder how he could have found it out?'
> If you have not yet fathomed the answer to her question, you must read the next chapter. (146–148)

Reaching into the outer layers of waking reality, Baoyu's exclamation interrupts the dream, calling the maids to come to his rescue. If this dream was devised to awaken Baoyu's virtue by means of a vision of existential emptiness, it fails. Like Weiyang Sheng, Baoyu is now caught in world of lust and merriment.

Fitting for a novel as complex as the *Dream*, this vision invokes the supernatural realm without offering answers. In spite of the narrator's promise, the reader never learns more about Baoyu's surprising knowledge of Qinshi's maiden name. Furthermore, the confusing blend of

Daoist-Buddhist nothingness and the utilitarian machinations behind Baoyu's erotic dreaming appear to be flawed by design. Disenchantment claims to speak from a privileged soteriological position yet appears surprisingly incompetent. In addition, the dream also features a cheeky passage that is congenial with Pu Songling's *Tales of the Strange*. Like Thoughtful Wang who makes an irreverent pun on the *Commentary of Zuo*, the dream narrative features a passage (paragraphs 1 and 2 of the above quote) in which the revered names of Confucius and Mencius are juxtaposed with the conventional metaphor for the sexual encounter, the 'joys of clouds and rain.' In the Neo-Confucian context, to reference the elevated sphere of the classical wisdom alongside base corporeality is highly transgressive. Huhua Zhuren (1805–1877), one of the great *Dream*-commentators of the 19th century, is half amused, half outraged by the passage: 'Through all the ages, what a strange thing to say! Through all the ages, what a strange text!'[5]

At first, the erotic dream does not trigger Baoyu's enlightenment but only his first nocturnal emission. In Chinese medicine, this is no laughing matter, as such events may lead to physical decay, even death. Consequently, the next chapter relates how his maidservant discovers 'something cold and sticky' (149) on the bedsheets and, after an initial moment of awkwardness, proceeds to repeat wit him 'the lesson he had learned from Disenchantment' (150). It turns out that Baoyu, the princeling, had this specific maidservant assigned with this purpose in mind in the first place. The idea is to prevent the physiological damages that would otherwise result from pubescent sexuality. For teenage boys who are subjected to strict Confucian morale, the lack of such preventive measures entails their exposure to existential danger. In the novel, this scenario is illustrated by the fate of Jia Rui, another boy of Baoyu's age. After falling in love with his cousin, the cunning Wang Xifeng, he finds his advances repeatedly rejected until he falls ill. Tied to the bed, he cannot stop masturbating, so his health keeps deteriorating. Eventually, as the relatives gather around his dead body, they discover a large puddle of ejaculate on his undergarments. The sensual dreams of his beloved have the same effect on the young man as the plots devised by spirit foxes who are intent on harvesting male *yang* energy.

The idea of the dangers of solitary sex, a recurring obsession in occidental culture,[6] is also found in Chinese medical beliefs. The reasoning, however, differs radically from the somatophobic concepts of the Judeo-Christian tradition. According to a treatise on the *Health*

Benefits of the Bedchamber (房中補益 Fang zhong bu yi), authored by the legendary medic Sun Simiao (581–682), the gold standard of sexuality is intercourse:

> Without woman, a man's mind will be disturbed; when the mind is disturbed, the spirit is wearied. [...] Forced repression [...] causes repletion of the [*jing*] and turns the urine turbid. It may even lead to the illness of copulation with ghosts.[7]

According to Chinese medical thought, *jing* (精) – next to *qi* (氣) and *shen* (神) – is one of the three essences of the body. The greatest strain on the body's *jing* resources is the production of sperm, but while this loss is compensated during proper sexual intercourse by one's partner's *jing* flow, solitary emissions unilaterally drain one's body.

Although the Fairy of Disenchantment's intention behind Baoyu's oneiric vision fails and inaugurates his sexual awakening rather than 'shocking the silliness out of him,' the operation succeeds in the long run. The book traces how illusion is first nurtured by the boy's carefree upbringing, then crushed by the kind of disappointment to which the fairy's name alludes. Baoyu's carefree youth comes to an end when he is strategically married off to Baochai while his true love interest, Daiyu, dies of consumption. Ultimately, no dream can have such a sobering effect as the experience of life itself – lest one considers the possibility that life itself is a dream.

Repression in Yu Dafu's novellas

In Chinese literary history, modernity arrived comparably late. At the onset of the 20th century, Chinese intellectuals sought to counteract the lingering feudal heritage, which was said to cause the population's passivity, moral decay, and its subjection to foreign rule. As writers turned to occidental philosophy and psychology for inspiration, Freudian dream analysis flourished in popular discourse and journal discussion, even long before *The Interpretation of Dreams* (*Die Traumdeutung*, 1899) appeared in full translation in 1932.[8] When transmitted across cultural barriers of understanding, however, such imports rarely produce carbon copies of foreign intellectual concepts. Consequently, in China Sigmund Freud became an emblem of a certain curiosity towards the dreamscape rather than the founding father of a specific methodology of interpreting dreams.[9]

Within the small pockets of literary experimentation between the fall of the Qing (1911) and the outbreak of the Civil War (1927–1949), Yu Dafu's and Guo Moruo's early works stand out for their frank portraits of sexually frustrated men who dream of romantic encounters. Their semi-biographical novellas address unfulfilled desires and articulate a general feeling of humiliation. Their dream visions owe much to Weiyang Sheng's tortured sexuality but have little in common with the ethics of moderation or grand metaphysical schemes that offer redemption.

Yu Dafu's novella *Boundless Night* tells of Zhefu, a young man who has recently returned from his studies in Japan. Although this impressionistic narrative hardly follows a clear trajectory, the main focus is on the transformations of his sexual drive, including phases of homoeroticism and masochism. As the personal narrator yields to inner monologue, Zhefu explains his resolutions upon returning to Shanghai: 'This time, I will thoroughly cleanse myself of those evil habits. I will stop smoking and drinking, and stop whoring around. I will work on my moral conduct and surprise my friends with how much I have changed.'[10] Back in his motherland, his unhealthy habits take a twist. Once he meets Chisheng, a pale young man suffering from pneumonia, Zhefu feels compensated for all past suffering. The narrator explains:

> During the ten years he spent roaming around Japan, he could not once satisfy his desire to love. Having met Chisheng, he felt he had finally encountered someone into whom he could freely pour his pent-up passion, someone with whom he could share his life's great events.[11]

Their tender affection is framed by literary references to the romantic relationship between the French poets Paul Verlaine and Arthur Rimbaud. The wording remains lofty: Zhefu's 'love' appears to denote purely spiritual feelings, as the physical component of their relationship remains concealed behind deflecting references. Their days of bliss are interrupted once Zhefu departs to a university job in Anqing. There, he is left to handle his libido alone once again. Now his carnal desire appears in his dreams in an uncensored fashion. Since this dream is also connected to an unpleasant encounter during daytime, the narrator takes this opportunity to examine the young man's inner life in psychological terms:

After his anxiety disappeared, Zhefu's self-esteem doubled and so did the familiar feeling that he had been insulted [i.e., by the school's dean]. And yet there was this natural force in him that undermined his self-esteem and taught him to endure the situation. Probably this is also the original drive behind his despicable acts. If he allowed this drive to grow inside him, it would become impossible not to develop a slave mentality (奴隸性質 nuli xingzhi). In our present society there are many successful people who only succeed because of such enslavement. Zhefu's moderately successful career so far relied on the slave mentality he demonstrated on this occasion.

Later in the evening Zhefu went to bed, his heart filled with two conflicting emotions. On the one hand, there was anxiety, primarily because he feared the students would not approve of him. On the other hand, there was joy because he was finally a teacher at a professional school. Just as he was thinking about this, he thought that someone slipped underneath his blanket. He closed his eyes and stretched out his hand to touch. It was Chisheng. He and Chisheng talked about many things in the most improper manner. The next morning, the servant came in to pour water for him to wash his face. He woke abruptly, only now realizing that he had been dreaming. When he rose he was still holding himself with two hands right there.[12]

Zhefu's erotic dream encounter with Chisheng is referenced in veiled terms. They only talk but in an 'improper' manner. There is no mention of sensual delights, yet his gesture upon waking indicates penile erection and a masturbatory intent. This dream encounter with an absent lover draws on Tang Xuanzu's *Peony Pavilion* but with a notable difference: here, the transgressive relationship is not between a human and a ghost but between two people of the same sex. While the ancient drama shows Liniang, who died of love, coming to life again after her soul repeatedly made love to Mengmei, Zhefu's oneiric encounter with Chisheng does not result in any tangible result – other than an erection. On a similar account, the novel does not culminate in their reunion but in despair.

In *Boundless Night*, Zhefu's psychological portrait differs considerably from the accounts of isolated modern souls, as found in occidental and Japanese modernism. He is not an atomized individual who has lost all moral and epistemic footing but remains a social being, even if this bond only shows in his 'slave mentality.' Advancing a free interpretation of Friedrich Nietzsche's term,[13] the narrative implies that Zhefu's inner turmoil is a phenomenon with sociopolitical significance. Life in a modern stratified society entails the psychological pressure of being subjected to hierarchical structures that reward submission. Consequently, the genesis of Zhefu's sexual repression is not tied to his early childhood, but connected to the structural makeup of society – a point that Wilhelm Reich indeed stressed and which brought him in conflict with Freudian orthodoxy.[14] Slave mentality, Yu implies, relates to social interactions, both as the prerequisite of successful careers and as the driving force behind 'despicable' acts.

Yu's text features a plethora of acts that transgress the realm of ordinary sexuality. If the dream articulates his pent-up anger in a comparatively soft way, Zhefu's sojourn at the academy facilitates other manifestations of his drives that are more unsettling. After failing to find himself a prostitute in the small town, he purchases a used needle and, after returning to his room, starts to prick his own face, triggering a wave of autoerotic sensations. Later, a colleague takes him to a brothel, where he comes up with an original preference: he asks for the oldest and ugliest woman with least customers. One can imagine Weiyang Sheng enjoying such waywardness – but Zhefu does not. Afterwards, he tells his colleague: 'I have already turned into a living corpse.'[15]

Import of guilt in Yu Dafu's and Guo Moruo's prose

Ruth Benedict's *The Chrysanthemum and the Sword* from 1947 popularized the idea that Japanese mentality differs from Judeo-Christian culture by its emphasis on shame over guilt. Although the concept of Japanese shame is contestable,[16] the book remains relevant as a reminder of the unintended effects of occidental modernity on the Far East. Arguably, guilt represents one of the key concerns in European and American letters, from which psychoanalysis also derived its nucleus: the idea of the individual's struggle with forces of the superego and the id.

By issuing translations of the occidental canon, literati helped introduce the concept of guilt to Japanese and, by association, Chinese readers. This trend thrived during the Japanese Meiji period (1868–1912), when many progressive intellectuals converted to Christianity, and left an indelible mark on Japanese letters.[17] Arguably, one of Japan's modern classics is the result of this transcultural grafting process, Natsume Sōseki's (1867–1916) *Kokoro* (1914). In this prose masterpiece, Sensei, an aging man, fails to come to terms with the guilt resulting from a friend's tragic suicide; as young men, they were in love with the same girl, and she opted for Sensei.[18] In China, this import of guilt is best exemplified in the prose of Yu Dafu and Guo Moruo, who became acquainted with Western letters while studying in Tokyo and Fukuoka.

In Yu's *Moving South*, the protagonist is on the verge of throwing himself into a carefree love story. But once the pangs of Christian guilt hit him, everything turns sour. Yiren, a young Chinese man, obsesses about Miss O, an innocent Japanese college student who is also a devout Christian. Having met at a church service, they go for long walks on the beach where she, to his great excitement, recites German poetry. Of all songs, she chooses *Mignon's Song*, a poem by Johann Wolfgang von Goethe, relating the story of an abandoned girl: 'You poor child, what have they done to you?'[19] After this song has acted as a first indicator of Miss O's fragility, Yiren reacts with shock when he joins her at the church and the minister elaborates on the commandment against adultery, as featured in the Sermon on the Mount (Mat. 5.27). Although they are both singles, he starts to panic, possibly because his Chinese upbringing associated sexuality with more permissive moral standards. This crash course in occidental guilt has a drastic effect on the young man, who is now haunted by eerie dream visions. In the following passage, Miss O's innocence is tainted considerably:

> After he went to bed, he felt there was a woman's voice calling him outside the door! He listened to it carefully; yes, it is indeed the voice of the one who sang Mignon's song! He ran out and followed her to the beach.... He looked at her.... She looked as pale as a dead person.... Then she turned around and walked to the woods. He immediately chased after her, but at the opening of the woods, he suddenly saw that lascivious woman who cheated him last summer walking out of the woods. With a painful 'Ah!,' he wanted to run home. But his two feet simply could not move! After some agonizing time, he woke up. A cold sweat set on his body. He could no longer go to sleep. He remembered what happened last summer.... [20]

This dream marks the advent of the Madonna-whore complex, an occidental invention, in Chinese letters. Under the influence of guilt, Miss

O's assumed innocence is undercut by visions of an evil seductress. Caused by a split between the affectionate and the sexual currents in male desire, Freud described this complex as a direct cause of oedipal and castration fears.[21] In Yu Dafu's work, however, there is no mention of Yiren's childhood trauma or anything that recalls the fundamental operations of psychoanalysis. Instead, there is something strangely arbitrary about Yiren's decision to overassimilate Christian values. Sensual inhibitions and self-loathing, recurring motifs in Yu's prose, resurface and force the protagonist to divert his erotic interest away from a tangible target. In the context of Yu's work, the Madonna-whore trope represents just another variation of troubled sexuality. Ultimately motivated by 'slave mentality,' his protagonists no longer seek direct sexual fulfilment but naturally gravitate towards situations that entail sexual frustration.

Another striking example of the imported occidental trope of guilt features prominently in Guo Moruo's *Caramel Girl*. Once again, the story is set in the prime location of Chinese humiliation, Japan. The narrator is a Chinese student – not celibate but married with children – who falls in love with a simple girl working in a candy shop. Since he never stops to talk to her, fearing that she would object to his Chinese nationality or laugh at his modest Japanese language skills, he becomes silently obsessed with her. A plethora of Western tropes are thrown into the field to stage and sustain her lure, ranging from invocations of the Virgin Mary and Aphrodite to Vicente Blasco Ibáñez's (1867–1928) novel *Woman Triumphant* (*La maja desnuda*, 1904) and, of course, Don Juan. Such romantic references culminate in a bizarre fantasy of what Spanish women are like; according to the narrator, they have their men whipped 15 times before consenting to a marriage proposal.

Instead of risking said lashes, however, the narrator keeps his guard up and avoids speaking to the shop girl directly. Finally, he makes her acquaintance – in a dream. Here, erotic desire and gothic horror intermix:

> As Virgo stood in the sky, I silently opened the back door and went into the dark alley. […] Eventually, I arrived at her store. The door was closed, the streets were already deserted, only the bars emitted the sounds of sleepy lute players and prostitutes. I lingered in front of her store for a while, my heart beating loudly. I pressed my body against the door and kissed the wood, where her eyes became clearly visible. Then I returned to the park, to the cliff where I sat during the daytime.

How strange! Out of the dark of night, from across the open street somebody was approaching. An indistinct white shape, probably a woman. My hair stood on end. The female shadow hesitated for a while, then walked towards me. She came very close and then stood still. 'It's her!' My heart knew. Instantly I jumped towards her and held her by the hands. She did not flinch.

- 'It's so late, why aren't you sleeping?'
- 'Oh, we close our shop at twelve, and now it's only two o'clock.'
- 'You worked the entire day, aren't you sleepy?'
- 'How should I sleep? I saw you during the daytime but didn't see you leave, so I thought I could find you here. After closing the shop, I just kept walking for nearly two hours.'
- 'Ah, that's very sweet of you! Let's sit down near the cliff. Are you cold?'
- 'No.'

We were sitting together near the cliff, when her face became really pale in the starry night, her eyes frighteningly black. I could distinguish her eyelashes, hair by hair. […]

She asked me: 'When you came here, were your wife and your kids asleep?'

I panicked and could not say a word.

- 'You don't have to conceal anything from me. I was always aware that you had a wife and kids. She is very kind, in this city everybody speaks well of her. […] Although you only recently paid attention to me, I have been aware of you for a long time, but you didn't pay much attention. Didn't you bring your eldest daughter to the store today?'
- 'That's right. I am so sorry!'
- 'No, I should be sorry. It's just … only …'
- 'Just what? Is it only me who loves you?'
- 'I am ready and willing.'
- 'My girl! (Suddenly, I knelt down in front of her legs and held her with both hands.) My girl! I love you, I am dying to love you! You let my heart say things that I cannot say! (I pulled her hands towards my chest.) Feel how hard it beats!'
- 'I know.' Her voice faded. Suddenly, I heard her sobbing: 'Ah, I am so sorry for your wife.' She suddenly leaned her head on

my shoulder, our lips glued together. We embraced tightly and trembled silently in the dark.

Eventually, she lifted me up so we sat next to each other again. She began to speak softly, saying that she was abandoned by her parents. She was never loved by anyone. Her mother was an unmarried aristocrat, but she does not know who her father was. The man who raised her took her away right after birth and received two thousand yen for bringing her up. This man only has an old mother, who never married and served at the court. The girl's story did not surprise me at all. Whoever meets her can tell she is of no humble origin.

She said that her foster father and his mother did not love her, they always treated her as a freak accident. All her life she never received love from anyone. I am the first one to ever love her.

During her confession, she embraced me lightly, then repeatedly said:

- 'I am so sorry for your wife. I am so sorry for her. But I can die, I would not have any regret!' This timid girl suddenly started kissing me passionately, she kissed my lips and my shoulders, my neck. 'Please don't forget me! Because I will never forget you, never leave you.' She pulled out my fountain pen so I could leave her a memory. I agreed, then she embraced my neck again and continued to kiss me. She pulled me closer: 'You must not forget me.' Then she turned around, ran to the cliff and jumped into the sea of darkness!
- 'Ah!' I gasped in surprise, trying to fetch her by the hand – I caught her. But it was Duanhua [i.e., his wife]. She woke up with a start, asked me what the matter was. I was so stupefied I could not give an answer. Why did I not die in my dream?[22]

The narrator's dream features a simple wishful fantasy and its reversal, the possession and loss of the desired girl. Plagued by the guilt of cheating on his wife, the dream proposes a drastic solution for the shop girl's allure: her suicide. After the feudal practice of polygamy, a core feature of Chinese male identity up until the late 19th century, became associated with China's backwardness,[23] writers turned to the romantic utopia – with a chilling effect. Instead of being able to balance romance and marriage they discovered, like occidental Romantics before them, the frustrating split between the two functions.[24] Finding it impossible to integrate the roles of husband and lover, Guo's protagonist eventually chooses the path of insanity. After leaving town for some time, he returns to the candy shop. Learning that the girl has moved away, he tries to kill himself by drowning but is saved. There is a rumour that his beloved has married. Now he buys a gun and takes up her trail: 'I am going to Tokyo to kill someone – even if it's only myself!'[25] Like so many Romantic heroes before him, the narrator becomes the victim of the transformation of libido into death drive.

While writers such as Lu Xun also focused on the unrewarding role of the artist's wife – as in his short story *Divorce* (離婚 Lihun, 1926) – Guo's fictions remain limited to the scope of male suffering. *Late Spring* (殘春 Canchun, 1922) revisits the constellation of *Caramel Girl* and puts forward another variation on the trope of the unhappily married Chinese man who moves to Japan to study. Again, the pitfalls of adultery evoke drastic dream images. When visiting a sick friend in the hospital, Aimou falls in love with his nurse. He stays for the night at his friend's place, who mentions to him that the beautiful nurse was born in America but lost her parents at a tender age when she was forced to move back to Japan. He also mentions that she is of weak health. As the narrator slowly drifts away to sleep, the report about her sad fate and his desire create a sultry dream that, once again, takes a gothic turn. He meets her on a mountain peak, where she confirms what his friend told him: she is an orphan and suffers from tuberculosis. Remembering that Aimou is a student of medicine, she asks him to heal her:

> 'Mr Aimou! Tell me outright! Tell me, does a good-for-nothing like me deserve to exist?...'
> 'Dear girl, don't be so sentimental. I don't mean to flatter you, but you have managed to make a living since you were still a child, you put everyone else to shame! If you are suffering from such a grave sickness, you should have it examined by a skilful physician. Don't worry so much, it will only compromise your health.'
> 'Mr Aimou, in this case, can you please examine me?'
> 'But I am still quite inexperience as a physician.'
> 'Oh, you don't have to be polite!,' she said and slowly undressed to reveal her chest. Her body was a marble statue, her shoulders sloping like peeled lychees. Her breasts stood up like two unopened rose buds. I got up and let her sit down. As she stared at me, I saw twin stars twinkling. I rubbed my hands together and started to

tap her chest. Out of breath Baiyang [i.e., Aimou's friend] came running and shouted:

– 'This is not good! This is not good! Aimou! Aimou! You cannot stay here! Your wife has killed both your kids!'[26]

On arriving home, he finds his wife with bloodied hands and the lifeless corpses of his children. With a start he wakes up. Telling his friend about the dream, he realizes: 'Ah! This is taken from the tragedy of Medea! I cannot stay any longer, I must return home! I must return!'[27] Subsequently, the narrator returns to his wife and children, who are safe and sound. Taking the cue from Freud, Guo draws on Greek mythology to frame psychological afflictions: just like Medea punishes unfaithful Jason by killing their children, the narrator's erotic check-up on the nurse is interrupted by his wife's heinous revenge. Notably, Guo does not refer to an analogous Chinese legend, such as Empress Wu Zetian's killing of her sons, but prefers an occidental model. Apparently, the stark images of subconscious life are better articulated in Greek imagery.

Conclusion

The corpus demonstrates great variability in terms of the drama that surrounds the sexual dream. In *Carnal Prayer Mat*, the pains of Buddhist asceticism, supposedly a cure against the karmic entanglements of the flesh, culminate in Weiyang Sheng's wet dream. The ensuing drastic act, his self-castration, is congenial to Christian saints, notably Origen of Alexandria (184–253), who underwent a similar procedure. This said, the narrator's ironic perspective on extreme acts, whether asceticism or debauchery, does not lend itself to devout imitation by readers. Medical and soteriological notions inform Weiyang Sheng's erotic dreams without providing clear moral guidelines that go beyond the recommendation to observe moderation. Within the narrative, such dreams interfere with the course of events – for better or worse.

In *Dream of the Red Chamber*, the machinations of Baoyu's ancestors devise an erotic dream meant to facilitate spiritual awakening, but it ultimately fails to change his attitude toward the 'serious things of life.' This said, one may argue that they succeed in the long run, as the value that he attaches to tender feelings and sensuality ultimately culminates in his personal tragedy and disillusion with the world. In contrast to moral message found in *Carnal Prayer Mat*, the complex causation that underpins Baoyu's erotic attachments goes far beyond the recommendation to observe moderation in all aspects of life. Arguably, *Dream of the Red Chamber* tests the limits of the oft-quoted analogy that life is but a dream. Once the narrative action takes place in a multi-layered cosmos, dreams lose their potential to upset reality, as the events taking place in each layer are deferred to yet other levels. Like in the *Zhuangzi*'s butterfly text, to tell the difference between the dream experience and the dreaming subject remains an utterly hopeless endeavour.

After the invention of the biographical subject in Chinese literature, writers formed themselves after the Romantic author concept shaped by occidental modern literature. The repressed sexuality of Yu's deviant singles and Guo's lusting husbands surfaces in dreams, including homosexual desires, masochistic drives, and the re-imagination of the beloved as Madonna-whore. Research literature often relates Yu's and Guo's protagonists to their authors' autobiographical confessions. This is regrettable, for it distracts from the sociopolitical nexus that departs markedly from European modernism's focus on the atomized soul's enstrangement from society at large. Yu's prose in particular culminates in the dejected individual's salvation through a transcendence of individualism, which shows most visibly in his much-discussed novella *Sinking* (沈淪, 1922). Here, the sexually tormented protagonist experiences his patriotic awakening towards the end.[28] In this context, erotic dreams participate in a new synthesis between the individual and the greater whole. As Chapter 5 will show, early Chinese modernism indeed generated a model of the psyche that allows the individual to participate in a spiritual union – through the collective national dream.

Notes

1 Li Yu, *The Carnal Prayer Mat*, trans. by Patrick Hanan (London: Arrow, 1990), 13. Henceforth quoted as CPM.
2 Patrick Henan, 'Foreword,' in: CPM vii–xiv, here x.
3 Wai-Yee Li, 'Early Qing to 1723,' in: *The Cambridge History of Chinese Literature*, ed. by Kang-I Sun Chang and Stephen Owen, 2 vols (Cambridge: Cambridge University Press, 2010), II, 152–244, here 208.
4 Susan Sontag, *Styles of Radical Will* (London: Secker & Warburg, 1969), 58.
5 Orig. '千古奇事，千古奇文。' Cao Xueqin 曹雪芹, *Dream of the Red Chamber: Three Commentaries Edition* (紅樓夢：三家評本 Hong lou meng: San jia ping ben), 3 vols (Shanghai: Shanghai guji chubanshe, 2007), I, 85.

Erotic dreams 85

6   See Thomas W. Laqueur, *Solitary Sex: A Cultural History of Masturbation* (New York: Zone Books, 2004).
7   Cited in: Douglas Wile (ed.), *Art of the Bedchamber: The Chinese Sexual Yoga Classics* (New York: State University of New York Press, 1992), 117–118.
8   See Chan, *The Edge of Knowing*, 20.
9   Many occidental poets shared this fate, for example Johann Wolfgang von Goethe, William Wordsworth, and Walt Whitman, as did philosophers, including Immanuel Kant and, significantly, Karl Marx and Friedrich Engels. See Changfu Xu, 'The Incomplete Transformation of Sinicized Marxism,' *Socialism and Democracy* 26.1 (2012), 1–17; Chenchen Tian, 'Mao Zedong, Sinicization of Marxism, and Traditional Chinese Thought Culture,' *Asian Studies* 7 (2019), 13–36.
10 Orig. '我這一次回國之後，必要把舊時的惡習改革得幹幹淨淨。戒煙戒酒戒女色。自家的品性上，也要加一段鍛煉，使我的朋友全要驚異說我是與前相反了。' Yu Dafu (郁達夫), *Selected Works* (精選集 Jing xuan ji) (Beijing: Yanshan chubanshe, 2011), 104. Henceforth quoted as YD.
11 Orig. '他在日本飄流了十來年，從未曾得著一次滿足的戀愛，所以這一次遇見了吳遲生，覺得他的一腔不可發泄的熱情，得了一個可以自由灌注的目標，說起來雖是他平生的一大快事。' (YD 106).
12 Orig. '恐懼的心思去了之後，質夫的自尊心又長了一倍，被侮辱的心思比從前也加一倍擡起頭來，但是一種自然的勢力，把這自尊心壓了下去，教他忍受了。這教他忍受的心思，大約就是卑鄙的行為的原動力，若再長進兒級，就不得不變成奴隸性質。現在社會上的許多成功者，多因為有這奴隸性質，才能成功，質夫初次的小成功，大約也是靠他這時候的這點奴隸性質而來的。這一天晚上質大上床的時候，卻有兩種矛盾的思想，在他的胸中來往。一種是恐懼的心思，就是怕學生不能讚成他。一種是喜悅的心思，就是覺得自家是專門學校的教授了。正在那里想的時候，他覺得有一個人鈷進他的被來，他閉著眼睛，伸手去一摸，卻是吳遲生。他和吳遲生顛顛倒倒的講了許多話。到了第二天的早晨，齋夫進房來替他倒洗面水，他被齋夫驚醒的時候，才知道是一場好夢，他醒來的時候，兩只手還緊緊的抱住在那里。' (YD 109–110).
13 By dropping the term 'slave mentality' into the narrative, Yu Dafu plays on Friedrich Nietzsche's (1844–1900) concept of slave morality, as elaborated on in *The Genealogy of Morals* (*Zur Genealogie der Moral*, 1877): 'weak' individuals or social groups rely on cleverness, disguise, and social connections to overcome the 'strong,' such as by repressing aggression and, at the same time, invoking moral superiority. Since the works of Nietzsche underwent similar transformations as those of Freud upon arriving in the Far East, this philosophical reference does not need to be overstressed. See Susanne Weigelin-Schwiedrzik, 'Das Leben im Schein

als Ziel: Lu Xuns *Wilde Gräser* und Nietzsches *Also sprach Zarathustra*,' in: *Konstellationen: Versuchsanordnungen des Schreibens*, ed. by Helmut Lethen, Annegret Pelz, and Michael Rohrwasser (Göttingen: Vandenhoeck & Ruprecht, 2013), 137–158.
14 For an account of Reich's combination of psychoanalysis and Marxism, see Bertell Ollman, *Social and Sexual Revolution. Essays on Marx and Reich* (Cambridge, MA: Southend Press, 1979), 176–204.
15 Orig. '我已經成了一個 Living Corpse 了。' (YD, 125). Latin script in the original.
16 See Millie R. Creighton, 'Revisiting Shame and Guilt Cultures: A Forty-Year Pilgrimage,' *Ethos* 18 (1990), 279–307.
17 See J. Scott Miller, *Adaptations of Western Literature in Meiji Japan* (London: Palgrave, 2001), 9–22.
18 See David C. Stahl, *Social Trauma, Narrative Memory, and Recovery in Japanese Literature and Film* (London: Routledge, 2020), 17–74.
19 Johann Wolfgang von Goethe, *Wilhelm Meister's Apprenticeship*, trans. by Eric A. Blackall (Princeton: Princeton University Press, 1995), 83.
20 Quoted and trans. in: Luying Chen, 'Translation and Feminization in Yu Dafu's *Moving South*,' *Rocky Mountain Review* 66.1 (2012), 45–63, here 54–55.
21 See David D. Gilmore, *Misogyny: The Male Malady* (Philadelphia: Pennsylvania University Press, 2001), 156–157.
22 Orig. "少女星高現在中天的時候，我一個人悄悄開了後門走出昏暗的巷道里來。… 我結局走到了她的店門了。門是緊閉著的，街上已經全無人跡，只有些酒食店里還有些饒有睡意的三弦和妓女的歌聲。我在她的店前立了一會，心子跳躍得發出聲響來，我貼身去在那門板上親了一吻，門板上分明是現著她的眼睛。我又走上園里，在我白天坐過的崖頭上坐下。 啊，奇怪！在這樣夜深的時候，從對面的路上公然還有人走來。模糊的白影，好象是一個女人，使我全身的毛根伸了幾下。女人的影子徙倚地漸漸向我走來，走到近處突然站立著了。"啊，是她！" 我心里這樣叫著，立刻跳起來跑去捉著她的兩手。她也沒有畏縮。— "這麼夜深你還沒有睡嗎？" — "唉，我們是十二點過才關的店門，現在不過是兩點鐘的光景。" — "你勞了一天怎麼不早睡呢？" — "我怎麼能夠睡呢，我自從白天看見你來，便沒有看見你回去，我猜你還是留在這園子里。我等關了店門便上這園子里來，我在這里徘徊了將近兩個鐘頭了。" — "啊，惹得你這樣關心！我們到崖頭去坐著說罷，你冷嗎？" — "不冷。" 我們兩人並坐在崖頭上，她的臉色在星光下看來是非常蒼白，眼睛是黑得怕人，睫毛是一根一根可以看得清楚。[...] 她問我："你來的時候太太和小姐們睡了沒有？" 我驚惶得說不出話來。— "你別瞞我，你是有太太和兒女的人，我早是曉得的。你的太太人很好，在H村住了兩年沒人不說她好的。[...] 你認識我好象是才不久的事情，但我是早認識你的，不過你不曾注意罷了。你今天帶來的不是你的大小姐嗎？"——"唉，唉，是的，是的。我對不起你！"——"倒是我對不起你呢。但是......只要......"——"只要什麼呢？只要我愛你麼？"——"唉，那樣時，我便死也心甘情願。"——"啊，姑娘！（我突然跪在她的膝前握著她膝上放著的兩手）啊，姑娘，姑娘！我愛你，我死心愛你，你讓我的心子來說我不能說出的話罷！（我把她的手引來按著我的心窩）你看它是跳得怎樣厲害，怎樣厲害喲！"——"我是曉得的。"她的聲音低沈了，結局帶著哭聲說道："啊，對不住你的夫人！"她突然把頭來垂到我的肩上，我們的嘴唇膠合著，兩人緊緊抱著，戰栗在無言的黑暗里。最後是她把我扶了起來，仍然坐在她的旁邊。她細細地說，她說她是生來便是被父母拋棄了的人。她沒有受過人的愛情。她的母親是一位未婚的貴族的處女，她的父親是什麼人，她現刻也還不知道。她現在的養父只是從她母姓的貴族得了二千圓的養育費抱繼過來的，剛在生下地時抱繼過來的。她的養父就只有一位老母，平生只是獨身。他的老母是那貴族家里的女婢。她說的這些話使我一點也不驚奇，無論什麼人看見她，都可以斷定她不是下賤人家的女子。她說：她的養父和祖母都不愛她，都只把她當成奇貨。她平生沒有受過別人的愛，她受我的愛情要算是有生以來的第一。她說著又把我緊緊擁抱著，連連叫道："對不住你的夫人，對不住你的夫人！但是我可以死，我是死無遺憾的了！"——"平常那麼嬌怯的女兒竟熱烈地向我親吻，吻了我的嘴唇，吻了我的眼睛，吻了我的肩，頸......你......你不要忘記我，我是死也不能忘記你的，我是死也不肯離開你！"她說著把我的一管自來水筆抽去，她要我給她做紀念。我答應了她。她又抱著我的頸子和我親了一吻，把手撒開了。"你不要忘記我。"說著便一翻身從崖頭向那深不可測的黑海里跳去！——"啊！"我驚叫了一聲，急忙伸手去抱她。我抱住了，但是，是我同床的瑞華！瑞華也驚醒了，她問我是怎麼一回事。我驚愕得一時回答不出來，......啊，我怎麼不死在夢里呢？' Guo Moruo 郭沫若, *Caramel Girl* (卡爾美夢姑娘 Kaermeimeng guniang) (Beijing: Shifan Daxue chubane, 1993), 67–68. Henceforth quoted as CM.

23 See Keith McMahon, *Polygamy and Sublime Passion: Sexuality in China on the Verge of Modernity* (Hawai'i: Hawai'i University Press, 2010), 1–2.
24 For a genealogy of occidental romance, see Eva Illouz, *Consuming the Romantic Utopia: Love and the Cultural Contradictions of Capitalism* (Berkeley: California University Press, 1997); Niklas Luhmann, *Love as Passion: The Codification of Intimacy* (Cambridge: Polity, 1986).
25 Orig. '我到東京去要殺人—至少要殺我自己！' (CM 81).
26 Orig. '"愛牟先生！你直說罷！你說，象我這樣的廢人，到底還有生存的價值沒有呢？......" "好姑娘，你不要過於感傷了。我不是對著你奉承，象你這樣從幼小而來便能自食其力的，我們對於你，倒是慚愧無地呢！你就使有什麼病癥，總該請位高明的醫生診察的好，不要空自擔憂，反轉有害身體呢。""那麼，愛牟先生，你就替我診察一下怎麼樣？" "我還是未成林的筍子呢！" "啊啦，你不要客氣了！" 說著便緩緩地袒出她的上半身來，走到我的身畔。她的肉體就好象大理石的雕像，她蟬著的兩肩，就好象一顆剝了殼的荔枝，胸上的兩個乳房微微向上，就好象兩朵未開苞的薔薇花蕾。我忙立起身來讓她坐，她坐下把她一對雙子星，圓睜著望著我。我擦暖我的兩手，正要去診打她的肺尖，白羊君氣喘籲籲地跑來，向我叫道："不好了！不好了！愛牟！愛牟！你還在這兒逗留！你的夫人把你兩個孩兒殺了！"' (CM 18–19).

27 Orig. '啊！這簡直是Medea的悲劇了！我再也不能久留，我明朝定要回去！定要回去！' (CM 20). Latin script in the original.

28 See Kirk Denton, 'The Distant Shore: The Nationalist Theme in Yu Dafu's Sinking,' *Chinese Literature, Essays, Articles, Reviews (CLEAR)* 14 (1992), 107–123, here 114; see also Shi Xiaoshi (施曉詩), 'The Development of Yu Dafu's Patriotism in *Sinking*' (從'沈淪'看郁達夫在愛國主義題材上的新開拓 Cong 'Chenlun' kan Yu Dafu zai aiguo zhuyi ticun shang de xin kaitu), *Yalüjiang Literary Monthly* (鴨綠江) 1 (2015), 56–63.

Bibliography

Cao, Xueqin (曹雪芹). *Dream of the Red Chamber: Three Commentaries Edition* (紅樓夢：三家評本 Hong lou meng: San jia ping ben), 3 vols (Shanghai: Shanghai guji chubanshe, 2007).

Chan, Roy Bing. *The Edge of Knowing: Dreams and Realism in Modern Chinese Literature* (Seattle: Washington University Press, 2017).

Chen, Luying. 'Translation and Feminization in Yu Dafu's Moving South,' *Rocky Mountain Review* 66.1 (2012), 45–63.

Creighton, Millie R. 'Revisiting Shame and Guilt Cultures: A Forty-year Pilgrimage,' *Ethos* 18 (1990), 279–307.

Denton, Kirk. 'The Distant Shore: The Nationalist Theme in Yu Dafu's Sinking,' *Chinese Literature, Essays, Articles, Reviews (CLEAR)* 14 (1992), 107–123.

Gilmore, David D. *Misogyny: The Male Malady* (Philadelphia: Pennsylvania University Press, 2001).

Guo, Moruo (郭沫若). *Caramel Girl* (卡爾美夢姑娘 Kaermeimeng guniang) (Beijing: Shifan Daxue chubane, 1993).

Illouz, Eva. *Consuming the Romantic Utopia: Love and the Cultural Contradictions of Capitalism* (Berkeley: California University Press, 1997).

Laqueur, Thomas W. *Solitary Sex: A Cultural History of Masturbation* (New York: Zone Books, 2004).

Li, Wai-Yee. 'Early Qing to 1723,' in: *The Cambridge History of Chinese Literature*, ed. by Kang-I Sun Chang and Stephen Owen, 2 vols (Cambridge: Cambridge University Press, 2010).

Li, Yu (李漁). *The Carnal Prayer Mat*, trans. by Patrick Hanan (London: Arrow, 1990).

Luhmann, Niklas. *Love as Passion: The Codification of Intimacy* (Cambridge: Polity, 1986).
McMahon, Keith. *Polygamy and Sublime Passion: Sexuality in China on the Verge of Modernity* (Hawai'i: Hawai'i University Press, 2010).
Miller, Scott J. *Adaptations of Western Literature in Meiji Japan* (London: Palgrave, 2001).
Ollman, Bertell. *Social and Sexual Revolution. Essays on Marx and Reich* (Cambridge, MA: Southend Press, 1979), 176–204.
Shi, Xiaoshi (施曉詩). 'The Development of Yu Dafu's Patriotism in *Sinking*' (從'沈淪'看郁達夫在愛國主義題材上的新開拓 Cong 'Chenlun' kan Yu Dafu zai aiguo zhuyi ticun shang de xin kaitu), *Yalüjiang Literary Monthly* (鴨綠江) 1 (2015), 56–63.
Sontag, Susan. *Styles of Radical Will* (London: Secker & Warburg, 1969).
Stahl, David C. *Social Trauma, Narrative Memory, and Recovery in Japanese Literature and Film* (London: Routledge, 2020).
Tian, Chenchen. 'Mao Zedong, Sinicization of Marxism, and Traditional Chinese Thought Culture,' *Asian Studies* 7 (2019), 13–36.
von Goethe, Johann Wolfgang. *Wilhelm Meister's Apprenticeship*, trans. by Eric A. Blackall (Princeton: Princeton University Press, 1995).
Weigelin-Schwiedrzik, Susanne. 'Das Leben im Schein als Ziel: Lu Xuns Wilde Gräser und Nietzsches Also sprach Zarathustra,' in: *Konstellationen: Versuchsanordnungen des Schreibens*, ed. by Helmut Lethen, Annegret Pelz, and Michael Rohrwasser (Göttingen: Vandenhoeck & Ruprecht, 2013), 137–158.
Wile, Douglas (ed.). *Art of the Bedchamber: The Chinese Sexual Yoga Classics* (New York: State University of New York Press, 1992).
Xu, Changfu. 'The Incomplete Transformation of Sinicized Marxism,' *Socialism and Democracy* 26.1 (2012), 1–17.
Yu, Dafu (郁達夫). *Selected Works* (精選集 Jing xuan ji) (Beijing: Yanshan chubanshe, 2011).

5 Collective national dreams

Sometimes, dreams guide the dreamer straight into the realm of politics. In the Chinese literary tradition, there exists a type of non-psychological dream that provides access to a transhistorical public sphere. Such dream visions can be experienced by powerful rulers and critical observers alike, who both find themselves treated to privileged insights into the workings of history, be it the laws of wise rule or the itinerary toward a prosperous future. In this function, collective dreams open the gates to a supranatural archive that is unspoiled by all-too-human machinations and short-sightedness. Unlike their rough Christian equivalents,[1] such dreams are neither facilitated by direct divine inspiration nor require personal repentance; instead, they seek to rectify the disjunction between the universal law and its implementation in the world of humans.

The intellectual grounding for this type of dream coincides with the arrival of a European idea in the East Asia: the nation state. As the failed reformers of the late nineteenth century turned to literary writing, collective national dreams emerged as an outlet for political frustration with the perceived incompetence of the Qing court. Liu E's *Travels of Lao Can* (老殘遊記 Lao Can you ji, 1903–1904) features a dream that contains a cautionary warning against the country's disorientation. Meanwhile, Wu Jianren's *New Story of the Stone* (新石頭記 Xin Shi tou ji, 1905/1908) goes into the opposite direction by offering a grand vision of the country's renaissance. Today, collective national dreams are still widely discussed, as the People's Republic of China uses dream rhetoric to legitimize its power. In this context, Ma Jian's *China Dream* (中國夢 Zhongguo meng, 2018) draws on the concept of collective national dreams to address the problematic aspects of a homogenized consciousness.

DOI: 10.4324/9781003481881-5

The Dao of Heaven

While most religions and cosmologies feature metaphysical interventions that aim to correct mankind's waywardness, the ruler's dream of Chinese antiquity is sourced from the Dao, an immanent cosmic force that is eternal and unchanging. As the ancient dreams described in Chapter 1 show, such dreams testify the interconnectedness between the human sphere and Heaven: the *Classic of Poetry* reports the ruler's prophetic dream about his offspring, *Records of the Great Historian* tell of Wu Ding who recruited his ministers through dream visions, and the *Liezi* reports that the Yellow Emperor visits Huaxu country in his dream and returns with supreme insights about statecraft. To different degrees, such dreams highlight that the ruler's life is in harmony with the cosmic force. the Dao of Heaven. According to the *Book of Documents* (書經 Shu jing, 4th c. BCE), one of the prime sources of Confucian philosophy, a perfect ruler achieves unity with his subjects by transcending his own personhood: 'Heaven sees as my people see; Heaven hears as my people hear.'[2]

Despite the unchanging nature of the Dao of Heaven, philosophers and historians have not failed to observe that it is distributed unequally among rulers across time. Sima Qian (145–87 BCE) explained such changes as the effect of the historical cycles which determine the rise and fall of every dynasty. While the beginning of a dynasty coincides with the unreserved Mandate of Heaven, the dynasty's ability to maintain this connection gradually decreases. Once a cycle nears its end, warning signs appear in the shape of civil unrest, natural disasters, and corruption.[3] Placed in the cyclical dynamics of history, collective dreams fall into a period of decline. When interpreted correctly, they can inspire efficient countermeasures and possibly inspire a renewal of the Mandate of Heaven.

The Qing empire's decline in *Travels of Lao Can*

Toward the end of the nineteenth century, the Qing empire found itself in a quagmire of crises, experiencing subsequent Western attacks on its territorial integrity and a tide of civil unrest that culminated in the Yihetuan Movement (1899–1901), also known as the Boxer Rebellion. Inevitably, the impression was that the Manchus' dynastic rule was nearing its end. Liu E, a multi-talented scholar and engineer, belonged to the most original observers of the Qing's woes. Although he belonged to the traditionalist camp that never dared to question the legitimacy of the imperial system itself, a business venture, realized with foreign capital, brought him in conflict with the central government to the effect that he was ordered into exile to Xinjiang. In *Travels of Lao Can*, he articulates his grievances in the form of an allegorical novel about China's place in the modern world.

The novel's protagonist, Lao Can, is characterized as a self-learned scholar who lacks the family connections and wealth required to become a man of distinction, so he travels the country curing rare illnesses. After a convalesced wealthy patron treats him to a grand feast, Lao Can overindulges in drinking and retreats to his room to have a rest. Here, he dreams of the country's bleak future, should it fail at striking the right balance between its traditional feudal heritage and new geopolitical challenges:

> On the day when our story begins Lao [Can] had finished his noon meal, and having drunk two cups of wine more than usual, felt tired and went to his room, where he lay down on the couch to rest. He had just closed his eyes when suddenly two men walked in, one called Wen [Zhangbo], the other [De Huisheng]. These two men were old friends of his. They said, 'What are you doing at this time of day, hiding away in your room? [...] We are going to [Dengzhoufu] to see the famous view from the [Penglai] Pavilion and have come especially to invite you.' [...]
>
> When they entered the pavilion, they sat at a table by a window and looked out toward the east. All they could see were white waves like mountains stretching away without end. [...] Around the pavilion the wind rushed and roared until the whole building seemed to be shaking. The clouds in the sky were piled up, one layer upon another. [...]
>
> [Zhangbo] meanwhile had been looking through his telescope. Now he exclaimed, 'Look! [...] Look at that sailing boat among the great waves. It must be in danger.' [...]
>
> After about an hour the boat was so near that by looking closely through their telescopes the three men could see that it was a fairly large boat [...]. The captain was sitting on the poop, and below the poop were four men in charge of the helm. [...] Countless people, men and women, were sitting on the deck without any awning or other covering to protect them from the weather – just like the people in third-class cars on the railway from [Tianjin] to [Beijing].

The north wind blew in their faces; foam splashed over them; they were wet and cold, hungry and afraid. [...]

It was a great ship, twenty-three or twenty-four [zhang] [i.e. a measuring unit, ca. 3.2 meters] long, but there were many places in which it was damaged. On the east side was a gash about three [zhang] long, into which the waves were pouring with nothing to stop them. Further to the east was another bad place about a [zhang] long through which the water was seeping more gradually. No part of the ship was free from scars. [...] [T]hey saw several people on the boat killed and thrown into the sea. The helm was put about, and the ship went off toward the east. [...]

Lao [Can] [said], 'As I see it the crew have not done wrong intentionally; there are two reasons why they have brought the ship to this intolerable pass. What two reasons? The first is that they are accustomed to sailing on the 'Pacific' Ocean and can only live through 'pacific' days. When the wind is still and the waves are quiet, the conditions of navigation make it possible to take things easy. But they were not prepared for today's big wind and heavy sea and therefore are bungling and botching everything. The second reason is that they do not have a compass. When the sky is clear, they can follow traditional methods, and when they can see the sun, moon, and stars they don't make serious mistakes in their course. Theis might be called 'depending on heaven for your food.' [...] [I]f we [...] follow them in a fishing boat, we can certainly catch them, because their boat is heavy and ours will be light. If when we have reached them we give them a compass, they will then have a direction to follow and will be able to keep their course.'

As Lao Can and his two friends close in on the ship, they see that its sailors are robbing the passengers. Meanwhile, agitators have started to whip up the passengers against the crew and urge them to kill those who are in charge of the ship. Eventually, the three go aboard:

Bowing very low, they took out their compass and sextant and presented them. The helmsmen looked at them and asked them politely, 'How do you use these things? What are they for?'

They were about to reply when suddenly among the lower ranks of seamen arose a howl, 'Captain! Captain! Whatever you do don't be tricked by these men. They've got a foreign compass. They must be traitors sent by the foreign devils! They must be

Catholics! They have already sold our ship to the foreign devils, and that's why they have this compass. We beg you to bind these men and kill them to avoid further trouble. If you talk with them any more or use their compass, it will be like accepting a deposit from the foreign devils, and they will come to claim our ship.'

This outburst aroused everybody on the ship. [...] 'These are traitors who want to sell the ship! Kill them! Kill them!'

When the captain and the helmsmen heard the clamor, they hesitated. A helmsman who was the captain's uncle said, 'Your intentions are very honest, but it is difficult to go against the anger of the mob. You had better go away quickly.'

With tears in their eyes the three men hurriedly returned to their little boat. The anger of the crowd on the big ship did not abate, and when they saw the three men getting into their boat, they picked up broken timbers and planks damaged by the waves and hurled them at the small boat. Just think! How could a tiny fishing boat bear up against several hundred men using all their force to destroy it? In a short time the fishing boat was broken to bits and began to sink to the bottom of the sea. [...]

[Lao Can] realized that there was no hope for his life. All he could do was to close his eyes and wait. He felt like a leaf falling from a tree, fluttering to and fro. In a short time he had sunk to the bottom. He could hear a voice at his side calling to him, 'Wake up, Sir! It is already dark. The food has been ready in the dining hall for quite a long time.' Lao [Can] opened his eyes in great confusion, stared around him, and said, 'Ay! After all it was but a dream.'[4]

At first, Lao Can's dream appears to lead him into familiar Daoist territory because Mount Penglai, mentioned at the beginning, is a prime location of Chinese mythology. But rather than finding a land made of gold and silver, rather than encountering glasses that never become empty and the secret of eternal life, he finds himself situated within a metaphoric realm that condenses the situation of contemporary China within a succession of maritime scenes. Here, Liu E closes in on a metaphor that was first used by Xunzi (c. 310–235 BCE), a Confucian philosopher, who argued: 'The ruler is the boat and the common people are the water. It is the water that bears the boat up, and the water that capsizes it.'[5] In Lao Can's quandary, the metaphor articulates acute worries about China's imminent future, as the observed ship is bound to capsize. The allegorical elements account for country's greatest challenges: starting with the holes in the ship's hull, pointing at territorial concessions to foreign powers; to the unruly crew, indicating the widespread corruption among officials; through to the agitators, a heterogeneous group comprised by rebels like the Big Sword Society and disgraced reformers like Liang Qichao. But most importantly, the captain represents the Emperor – or much rather: the Empress Dowager Cixi (1835–1908), steering the country's fate since 1861. Used to more favourable weather conditions, the captain, lacking proper navigations tools, turns out to be ill-equipped to master the storm. Everything that used to work in benign and peaceful weather no longer suffices to steer the ship safely from port to port. As it turns out, the metaphorical boat is nothing more than a decorative Dragon Boat, ill-equipped to meet the challenges of the present (see Figure 5.1).

According to Lao Can, it does not follow that the captain needs to be replaced, but that he must gain access to working instruments. The dramatic climax shelters him from blame; after all, he is in fact willing to adopt new methods to overcome the crisis. The incentive to thwart Lao Can's plan origins among 'the lower ranks of seamen' who want to see all foreign goods prohibited, including the life-saving compass. It seems quite ironic, however, that *Travels of Lao Can* refer to the compass, in fact a Chinese invention, as of Western origin.[6]

Placed in the introductory chapter, the dream's programmatic message is that modern China's main challenge consists of a gradual readjustment of its cultural heritage to modernity, which must also include concessions to 'Western learning.' In contrast to Japan's Meiji Emperor, who subjected his empire to a process of radical modernization, China looked at occidental models with great suspicion. Except for a short spell of reformism, the Hundred Days' Reform (1898), the Empress's court found Western knowledge incompatible with the primacy of classical learning.[7] In this respect, the novel gives a wishful account of Empress Cixi's attitude towards modernization. Quite in contrast to the ship's captain, she considered the Yihetuan Movement – that is, the angry mob in Lao Can's dream – a tool that could be used to fight back foreign imperialist aggression. Enjoying the moral support of the imperial court, the grassroots movement intensified their attacks on foreign settlements, including the slaughtering of Christian missionaries and their Chinese converts. In the long run, however, the court's alliance with the popular uprising contributed to one of the darkest moments of the Imperial Age. When the Eight-Nation Alliance

96 Collective national dreams

Figure 5.1 Dragon Boat Race by the Baojin Hall by Wang Zhenpeng (detail). Ink on paper, Yuan dynasty. National Palace Museum (Taipei). Licensed under CC BY 4.0.

retaliated, they subjected the country to an orgy of violence and humiliation. Lao Can's enthusiastic vision of Western blessings turns a blind eye on the irrational vandalism that foreign powers exhibited on various occasions, including the destruction of Summer Palace in 1860 and the looting of Beijing in 1901.

When Lao Can wakes up with the classical formula 'After all it was but a dream!', the protagonist has little reason to stop worrying about the country's future. His journey takes him through provinces of great natural and poetic beauty but they are also haunted by the tyranny of local officials. Although he succeeds in rescuing wretched individuals occasionally, all his attempts to act for the common good on a more comprehensive scale, such as his recommendations for prudent flood prevention, are rejected by those who are in power. Ultimately, the novel articulates a 'deeper disquiet over the futility of individual action,'[8] as C.T. Hsia rightfully observed.

Yet the text also features a narrative insertion that gives rise to optimism, Shin Ziping's travel account of Peach Blossom Mountain in Chapters Eight to Eleven. Scholars have described this segment as 'totally detachable from the main narrative'[9] or as compromised addition by the text's editor;[10] strikingly, Yang Xianyi and Gladys Yang's translation even omits those chapters altogether.[11] Nonetheless, the segment holds the key to balancing the novel's overall sense of doom with its lyrical and humorous tone. As Shen Ziping, a young scholar, enters the supernatural realm of Peach Blossom Mountain, the philosopher girl Yugu and the prophet Yellow Dragon give recommendations on how the Confucian tradition could be saved, such as by establishing the equality of the sexes. Most significantly, the Yellow Dragon also makes a prophecy about future events that will turn the tide: '[1924] will be a time of real independent cultural harvest. After that the introduction of new culture from Europe will revivify our ancient culture of the Three Rulers and Five Emperors, and very rapidly we shall achieve a universal culture. But these things are still far off, not less than thirty or fifty years.'[12] With substantial delay, argues the Yellow Dragon, China inaugurates a period of cultural assimilation to Western modernity. Fittingly, the novel's editor, fearing reprisals for this radical vision, reframed Chapters Eight to Eleven as a dream.[13] Arguably, this intervention achieved quite the opposite, for dreams do not necessarily reduce the significance of what is said but emphasize its visionary qualities. In this light, the Peach Blossom Mountain segment functions as the optimistic counterpart of the pessimistic opening dream.

Dreaming China's rise in *New Story of the Stone*

Like Liu E, Wu Jianren belonged to the camp of scholars who worried that traditional learning was becoming increasingly obsolete in late-Qing life; but unlike Liu, Wu exhibited a more cautious perspective on the benefits of adopting Western ways. In *New Story of the Stone*, written in 1905 and amended in 1908, the author explicitly invokes Cao Xueqin's *Dream of the Red Chamber* as an intertextual source, which also circulated under the title *Story of the Stone* (石頭記 Shi tou ji). The Qing period indeed abounds with continuations of *Story of the Stone*, but while an overwhelming majority centres on neutralizing its tragic end,[14] Wu uses the protagonist to a more original purpose: Jia Baoyu, the adolescent aristocratic protagonist, wakes up in Shanghai of 1900. To his great shock, Baoyu finds himself in a thoroughly transformed country, where the Chinese people are allocated an inferior position within the city's ethnic hierarchy. Witnessing colonial aggression, rampant corruption, and misrule in Shanghai, he soon turns from a puzzled time traveller into a fervent Chinese nationalist who rejects the country's excessive import of foreign products, such as watches and phonographs. He jeers at his fellow countrymen: 'Foreigners' piss is all so fragrant. It's a pity I was never lucky enough to be a foreigner's dog and never had an opportunity to drink it.'[15]

The gritty stetting of *New Story of the Stone*, however, ends after 20 chapters. In the second half of the book, Baoyu embarks on a journey into the 'Civilized Realm,' a utopian alternative reality that is vaguely located in Shandong Province. Chinese engineers have outcompeted Western scientists by taking inspiration from ancient knowledge, as the main means of transport are sophisticated flying machines. Furthermore, the people's degree of self-cultivation has reached such a high degree that institutionalized religion has disappeared altogether. Everything comes together in the last chapter, when Jia Baoyu, the most prolific dreamer in Chinese literature, falls asleep. He embarks on a journey that conveys a glorious vision of the country's long-term future:

> Baoyou was tossing and turning and could not sleep, so he sat up and repeatedly lay down again. Just as his mind was drifting away, he saw a boy come in with a letter, saying: 'The messenger is waiting for your reply.' [...] Baoyu asked the boy: 'Where is the

messenger?' The boy said: 'Outside.' Baoyu got up and went outside, where he found Huang Fu. Huang Fu saw Baoyu, came closer to pay his respects and said: 'My humble self is asking Uncle Bao to come to Shanghai, it is urgent.' Baoyu said: 'Let me call a flying cart.' Huang Fu said: 'There's no need for a flying cart, there's already a horse waiting here.' Baoyu saw that there were indeed two horses ready, so he mounted one, and Huang Fu followed on the other one. As he gave free rein to the horse, it sprinted off as if chasing after wind and lighting. It passed several high mountains, repeatedly ran through thistles and thorns, then arrived at the sea where a boat was floating. [...] [O]n the water it continued its gallop, now traversing the waves. Baoyu rejoiced, himself releasing the reins so that his own horse could also trot on water. He secretly thought: I have heard the Thousand-Miles-Horse could tread on water and ascend mountains as if it were a plain. I didn't believe it, but there it is!

Both horses raced for some time until they arrived in Shanghai. Wu Bohui received them joyously, made a few casual remarks, then Baoyu asked what matter was so urgent. But Bohui laughed: 'There's nothing really urgent at all, it's just that we haven't seen each other in such a long time. I invited you to have a little chat and to take you to travel around the world.' Baoyu said: 'Since I got to the Civilized Realm, I considered the Chinese sphere as the most perfect thing, so what's the point of going anywhere else?' Bohui said: 'Didn't you know, since you left, a lot has happened. After the Empress Dowager Cixin and Emperor Guangxu [i.e. her underage son] returned to Beijing [after fleeing from the Eight-Nation Alliance], they formed a new government which resembled [the Hundred Days Reform of] 1898 very much. This said, while in 1898 policies were implemented with the power of a thunderbolt and the speed of lightning, this time they proceeded slowly, so you wouldn't see great results at first. In reaction to Americans prohibiting Chinese from entering the country, [...] Chinese merchants and scholars negotiated a boycott prohibiting the use of American goods. After taking off in Shanghai, every province and region followed [...]. When the news spread to Beijing and the government heard the news, they knew that it could count on the Chinese people's spirit!' [...]. Instantly, Baoyu saw himself placed on a steamer, and that steamer moved at an incredibly fast pace. Both riverbanks abounded with tall buildings, the chimneys formed

100 *Collective national dreams*

> a forest, until Baoyu said to himself: 'Where is this? I have never been here before.' Suddenly, he heard Bohui behind his back: 'This is the Yangtze River!' Baoyu turned his head: 'Both banks of the Long River, are there so many buildings? Bohui said: 'Don't you know? Today, from Wusong up to Hankou, both banks are continuously lined with Chinese factories.'[16]

This brief historical review argues that one of the most humiliating episodes of the late-Qing era, the capture of Beijing by the Eight-Nation Alliance in 1901, was a direct consequence of the court's rejection of reforms. Having learned her lesson, Empress Cixi now embraces modernization and even adopts nationalist policies, such as a boycott of American imports. Baoyu's river cruise showcases one of the most tangible long-term consequences of such policies: the entire Yangtze River is studded with factories. Baoyu's vision does not stop here, but proceeds to demonstrate China's renaissance as a geopolitical superpower:

> In the blink of an eye, the steamer had arrived Hankou. [...] Raising his head, he saw an incredibly tall building next to the street with an empty plaza in front. In the middle stood a flagpole high as the heaven with the yellow flag of the flying dragon fluttering in the wind. There was also a long rope [...] hoisting the flags of all five continents and all the nations. The entrance of the building carried five characters that read: *All-Nations Peace Conference* in golden engraving, flashing in the sunlight, dazzling the eye. Baoyu strolled into the building, realizing that it hosted a big conference packed with Chinese and foreigners, he could not tell how many people there were. They were waiting for a long time already but remained silent. Then a bell sounded, and Baoyu heard a voice next to himself: 'The chairman will step on the stage now, it's the Chinese Emperor.' [...] As he turned his eyes to the stage, the man who stood on the podium turned out to be Dongfang Wenming [東方文明, literal meaning: Oriental Civilization]. He said: 'Today, on the first day of the All-Nations Peace Conference, every nation elected us to act as President. [...] This peace conference seeks to achieve peace for the globe's entire humanity, for every government. We all shoulder the responsibility to protect peace. We will ensure that every people is treated as equals without exception, including reds, blacks, and brown people. One cannot tyrannize their governments

and their people. [...] In respect of the unlearned peoples, we have the responsibility to guide and encourage them [...]. After this conference, we will eliminate power politics and advance pacifism.' The entire hall was filled with applause. Baoyu clapped his hands untiringly, then started to stomp with his feet. But who would have guessed that his feet treaded in the void, he fell thousand zhang, at once his eyes only saw darkness and his body started to break out in cold sweat. Forcing his eyes open, he found himself sleeping in a bed at Dongfang Wenming's house. It turned out all was a dream.[17]

After waking up from this dreamworld, Baoyu finds himself in the Civilized Realm again. The novel abruptly draws to a close amid a thicket of intertextual borrowings from the original *Story of the Stone*, leaving the triangulation between Shanghai of 1900, the Civilized Realm, and the dreamscape unresolved.

Wu Jianren's vision of a powerful China raises a number of questions, starting with the racial ideas that inform the Emperor's speech. Despite his professed pacificism, he contradicts his demand that every people should be treated as equal; after all, he arrogates his country's authority to guide and encourage the 'unlearned people.' Hereby, the Emperor, who bears the aptronym 'Oriental Civilization,' reasserts the sense of cultural superiority that China had enjoyed for thousands of years before facing the British navy in the First Opium War (1839–42). Quite in contrast to the ancient Confucian conviction that civilization comprises a set of cultural attributes that can be adopted by different groups, late-Qing reformers like Yan Fu and Liang Qichao popularized the idea of a racial hierarchy, in which the 'yellow' and the 'white' races dominate the world, while the 'red,' the 'brown,' and the 'black' hold an inferior position.[18] As Frank Dikötter's study shows, the logical conclusion of Yan's and Liang's adaptation of social Darwinism also implied that the leading races, 'whites' and 'yellows,' were supposedly facing an existential battle for supremacy at the onset of the twentieth century. Although Wu Jianren's narrative does not elaborate on these particulars, the Chinese Emperor's position as the unquestioned leader of the world and his declared mission to guide the disenfranchised races is unambiguous about the outcome of such racial struggle.

From a narrative standpoint, there is no need to frame this hypothetical future as a dream. Although many utopian novels start with a dream scenario or mark the departure into fantasy with one, the final chapter is thoroughly confusing, as the dream is awkwardly inserted into the Civilized Realm, in itself a utopian vision. Although both relate desirable aspects of China's future, the dream draws an even more glowing picture, as advanced technical devices such as flying carts are mentioned alongside mythical creatures, such as the Thousand-Miles-Horse. The juxtaposition of technological and mythical elements makes the achievements of the dream realm appear somewhat fragile, which is why David Wang argues that the dream sequence's purpose is to remind readers of the remoteness and inaccessibility of the perfect Chinese order.[19]

Contrary to this pessimistic line of interpretation, the present chapter claims that the insertion of a dream sequence into an already utopian setting in fact points to the text's double cultural matrix. While the utopian elements in *New Story of the Stone* are in parts derived from Western utopian novels that embrace technological progress, such as Edward Bellamy's *Looking Backward* (1888) and Alexander Craig's *Ionia* (1898), the final dream sequence wilfully breaks with their conventions. This narrative trick is a concession to the kind of visionary dream that moves beyond the life of the individual and draws its legitimacy from the Dao of Heaven. After Chapters One to Twenty have portrayed China as a country in decline, Baoyu's concluding dream shows that a new cycle of history is about to begin; once the Empress installs a new government, the Mandate of Heaven will be regained. In this context, the appearance of the Thousand-Miles-Horse marks the country's return to imperial splendour rather than pointing at the fragile fictionality of the oneiric construct. As the Chinese civilization moves into a new phase, the Emperor can proclaim that the past and the future collapse in a glorious period of peace.

State-sponsored harmony in *China Dream*

Fast-forward to the year 2022. When reading Wu Jianren's dream vision of a powerful China today, one cannot fail to notice that many aspects have become true, starting with the transformation of the Yangtze River's banks into industrial sites to the country's geopolitical status as a world power. Its leaders have started to shape the world in their image, as they portray China's peaceful rise as an alternative to American leadership. Arguably, the delicate balance between falling behind and full-scale Westernization, the main theme of *Travels of Lao Can* and *New Story of the Stone*, is done justice: Western knowledge was duly accepted as integral for socio-economic development, yet the sense of Chinese uniqueness was never lost, neither during the socialist decades, when Mao Zedong advanced his own take on Marxism-Leninism, nor during the period of authoritarian capitalism, which is officially designated as 'Socialism with Chinese Characteristics' (中國特色社會主義 Zhongguo tese shehui zhuyi). The realization of such dream goals, however, did not upend the use of oneiric imagery in political and literary fiction of the country. Although the collective national dream disappeared from literary expression by the end of the Qing era, the dream metaphor has re-emerged as a central ideological innovation of recent years.

In 2012, when Xi Jinping assumed the position of General Secretary of the Chinese Communist Party, he conjured the concept of the 'Chinese Dream of National Rejuvenation,' an opaque formula that is now firmly established as the country's central national narrative. Hereby, Xi reclaims the dreamer's perspective as the king's. Like the Yellow Emperor of the *Liezi*, the implication is that Xi has obtained the Mandate of Heaven to create a perfect society.[20]

Chinese writers did not fail to take note of the formula's impact on collective memory. After all, the dream rhetoric emerges against the backdrop of the Party's murderous policies that had cost millions of lives in the twentieth century and, simultaneously, its cynical rehabilitation of the Cultural Revolution as a period of resilience, perseverance, and success.[21] In reaction, contemporary novelists themselves adopted dream-themed narratives to reclaim the collective memory from political instrumentalization. On the one hand, this includes novels that are sold and published on the Chinese mainland, such as Fang Fang's *Soft Burial* (軟埋 Ruan mai, 2016), which tells of an amnesic old woman who recovers the memories of the atrocities committed during the Land Reform Movement of the 1950s. And on the other hand, this also applies to the political commentaries articulated by Chinese dissidents like Ma Jian who live in exile. His most recent novel, *China Dream*, gives a satirical account of the manipulation of the national collective dream by the state apparatus, thereby offering a counter-narrative to state-endorsed ideas of collective dreams.

The novel follows the rise and fall of Ma Daode, a high-ranking bureaucrat and ardent believer in the Chinese Dream. After the end of the Cultural Revolution, his career takes a stellar trajectory, eventually making him municipal leader and director of the 'Dream Bureau' in Ziyang, a fictional province. Today, his ambition is to develop a technological device to synchronize the population's dreams with the central government's requirements. Since the Chinese Dream is itself an elusive concept, Ma's overzealous attempts to establish himself as a reliable politician requires a delicate balance between propagandistic parlance and sheer madness:

> [T]his Ma Daode who grew up in the Cultural Revolution, this high official charged with promoting the great China Dream that will replace all private dreams, is afraid that his job will become imperilled. His past self and present existence are as antagonistic to one another as fire and water.
> At this morning's meeting, he got carried away. 'Our new president, Xi Jinping, has set forth his vision of the future', he told the assembled twenty-seven members of staff. 'He has conjured up a China Dream of national rejuvenation. It is not the selfish, individualist dream chased by Western countries. It is a dream of the people, a dream of the whole nation, united as one and gathered together into an invincible force. We have been urged to press ahead with indomitable will. Our job, in this Bureau, is to ensure that the China Dream enters the brain of every resident of Ziyang City. It seems clear to me that if the communal China Dream is to fully impregnate the mind, all private remembrances and dreams must first be washed away. And I, Ma Daode, volunteer to wash my brain first. I suggest we start work straight away on developing a neural implant, a tiny microchip, which we could call the China Dream Device. When the prototype is ready, I will insert it into my head, like this, and any dream from my past still lingering there will vanish into thin air...'
> At this, he stood up and mimed pushing the microchip into his ear.[22]

Originally conceived as a handy tool for top-down rule, Ma finds himself in desperate need of this fantastical device. Dividing his attention between official work and a dozen girlfriends, his scattered mind struggles to remain in control over his thoughts. His determination to supress the horrific memoirs of the time when he joined the Red Guards is not enough to keep at bay central episodes of his life:

Why am I being haunted by all these flashbacks, all these dreamlike visions of death and violence? The past and the present keep colliding in his mind. Last night, he dreamed of a place he has never seen before. It was a hospital corridor. Both walls were painted green on the lower half and a line of white ants was crawling along the dark crimson floor. At the end of the corridor was a room where the China Dream Bureau documents were stored. He opened the door and saw himself, sitting head bowed in front of a screen, typing the Bureau's annual report, his body shrouded in furry white mould. He could hear children playing basketball outside, and could smell the stench of rot wafting from his decaying double. Then, suddenly, he saw a body with a slashed cheek, staring straight at him, blood spewing from his mouth. Wendi [i.e. his wife] pinched his nose, trying to wake him up, and whispered, 'What did you say? Whose death do you want to avenge?'

Mao Daode glances over the leftover fish bones and charred beans lying on the table, and remembers the canteen of Yaobang Village School. It wasn't a real canteen – just a small room with a stove in the mud house of a villager who had been killed in the crossfire during the battle on the river front. Two hundred East is Red recruits [i.e. a faction of the Red Guards] were sent to that battle armed with just four hand grenades each. Only thirty returned alive.

Before he steps out of the front door, Ma Daode looks into the hallway mirror, presses an imaginary gun to his head, and says to himself: 'Hurry up and make the China Dream Device so that all these bloody nightmares can be erased.' (CD 34–35, emphasis in the original)

Both scenes show a man desperate to rid himself of the unwelcome memories that endanger the life he built as a party careerist. He only has two ways to save himself: should the China Dream device fail him, he is left to commit suicide.

The novel humorously exploits Ma's split identity on occasion of his visit of the Red Guard Nightclub, a Cultural Revolution-themed brothel, where he reconnects with his past by singing Revolutionary Songs during sexual intercourse. During daytime, however, psychopathological symptoms make him unable to carry out his duties as a party official such as when he unintentionally references the atrocities of the past in a public speech. Toward the end, the innermost source of his trauma surfaces: the double-suicide of his parents. It turns out that Ma himself denounced their bourgeois lifestyles, to the effect that his fellow Red Guards subjected them to savage beatings and humiliation.

China Dream offers a satirical perspective on the individual mind as a connecting node between the centralized state's efforts to repress individual memories and the uncontrolled return of those memories. Ultimately, this psychological antagonism also represents the clash that plays out between a premodern anthropology that assumes the existence of a suprahistorical sphere and modern psychology's scepticism toward non-personal memories. While the Party requires premodern subjects for its utopian vision of the future, its own members cannot escape the fate of post-Freudian souls. In this light, it is not surprising that Ma Daode, alarmed that his China Dream device will remain a pipe dream, resorts to a premodern myth to relieve the pressure on his troubled mind. After consultation with a witch doctor, Ma sets out to collect the ingredients required to brew the 'Old Lady Dream's Broth of Amnesia,' a soup served to dead souls before they reincarnate again. Hoping that the medicine delivers on the desired results, he plans to supply the supernatural drink to the entire Chinese population: 'Then I'll set up a China Dream Pharmaceutical Plant to manufacture Old Lady Dream's Broth, and my name will go down in history' (CD 86).

Ma's desperate search for a technological or pharmaceutical aid to restore the unity between ruler and the population articulates the absurdity of metaphysical politics in the twenty-first century. The Dao of Heaven may indeed accord with the lofty aims of peaceful and just government, yet this suprahistorical agent must overwrite and displace individual hopes and grievances. Both in antiquity as in the present, collective dreams come with the bitter taste of tyranny.

Conclusion

Collective national dreams require no psychological or spiritual explanation; they themselves make sense of the world by signalling the path that will lead from a frustrating present into a glorious future. In contrast to most prophetic dreams, not to mention psychological dreams, they envision a better world for the community to which the dreamer belongs, be it a ruler or a critical observer, forms part. Through the collective national dream, Chinese literati conveniently bridged one of the most significant dilemmas of occidental aesthetic

Collective national dreams 107

theory. Two decades after Liu E and Wu Jianren wrote down their collective dreamscapes and at the same time when Yu Dafu connected individual suffering with the fate of the nation, Georg Lukács addressed the fundamental disjunction between individual and society in the West. Modern literature, he argues, emerges from this state of forlornness: 'The epic individual, the hero of the novel, is the product of estrangement from the outside world.'[23] The implication is that any novel that pretended it could mend this rupture in a non-ironic manner would inevitably fail. In the Chinese context, however, the oneiric realm facilitated the emergence of a new union between individual and state.

When understood in primarily political terms, such dreams can completely dispense with the oneiric sphere. This is the case with the American Dream or the dreams articulated by the Civil Rights Movement, where the focus lies on socio-economic aspects and social justice alone. In the Chinese context, the dream-themed quest for community never lost its connection to the dream as a complex human activity. The cultural imaginary of antiquity, exemplified by the *Liezi*'s dream of the Yellow Emperor, concedes the dreamer privileged access to understanding the Dao of Heaven's correct application in the mundane realm. In Liu E's *Travels of Lao Can*, the protagonist's vision draws attention to the symptoms of an empire in decline. Faced with the apparent chaos that imperils the ship, Lao Can channels the Dao of Heaven by articulating straight-forward countermeasures that would boost the ship's ability to steer through the storm. Disappointingly, the time for China to achieve a 'universal culture' – that is, to abandon its self-centred culturalism – has not yet come. While the cycles of history proceed, the sage is condemned to the role of a passive observer. Meanwhile, Wu Jianren's *New Story of the Stone* offers a different take on China's decline, which can only be remedied by the patriotic awakening of the population. Once the Chinese people embrace the imaginary community of the nation state, they shall triumph in the struggle with other races for global domination. Eventually, the people's self-cultivation, engineering feats like flying cars, and the reappearance of mythological animals will herald a new period of Chinese supremacy.

The antagonism between Liu's cosmopolitan idealism and Wu's nationalism points at a fundamental problem behind visionary community-building, as not all people share the projected vision of utopia. After the collective national dream hatches from its humble origins in late-Qing utopian novels, Xi Jinping's *Dream* formula marks the end of visionary dreaming. In the media society of the twenty-first century, the new Yellow Emperor no longer asks to become the recipient of visionary dreams which would equip him with supreme insights into statecraft; instead, he enforces anaemic dreaming for his population. Taking into account the push for collective amnesia in contemporary China, a troubling aspect of the *Liezi* comes to light. The narrative describes the people of Huaxu as not only without cravings and lusts, but also as 'incapable of delighting in life or hating death.' The Daoist ideal of an indifferent population appears in an entirely different light when considering how desirable this ideal must appear to zealous bureaucrats like Ma Daode – or paramount leaders like Xi Jinping. In the twenty-first century, a population that no longer seeks to assert its civil liberties has not achieved peace of mind but is deprived of its political agency. The perfected country of old becomes a blueprint for the nightmare of totalitarian technocratic rule.

Considering the insights of ancient Chinese medicine which found that excessive dreaming throws *yin* and *yang* energies out of balance, one wonders what this Chinese Dream will bring for the future. Since the principal dreamer has become a geopolitical superpower, the consequences of his nocturnal emissions may have catastrophic effects on this dust-stained world of ours.

Notes

1 In the Judeo-Christian tradition, this kind of dream convinces Constantine the Great to convert his empire to Christianity.
2 James Legge (ed.), *The Sacred Books of China: The Texts of Confucianism*, trans. by J. L., 2 vols (Oxford: Clarendon Press, 1879), I, 128.
3 See Zvi Ben-Dor Benite, 'Long Divided Must Unite, Long United Must Divide: Dynasty, Histories, and the Orders of Time in China', in: *Power and Time: Temporalities in Conflict and the Making of History*, ed. by Dan Edelstein et al. (Chicago: University of Chicago Pres, 2020), 147–173, here 157–160.
4 Liu T'ieh-yün (劉鐵雲) (=Liu E), *The Travels of Lao Ts'an*, trans. by Harold Shadick (Ithaca, NY: Cornell University Press, 1952), 5–12.
5 Hsün Tzu (荀子), *Basic Writings*, trans. by Burton Watson (New York: Columbia University Press, 1969), 37.
6 Unlike the steam engine, the compass was already used in navigation in China from the 9th or 10th century onwards. See Joseph Needham, *The Shorter Science and Civilisation in China*, 5 vols (Cambridge University Press, 1980–1995), III, 176.

7 Influential scholars and educators like Woren (倭仁) (1804–1871) ensured that the Emperor's curriculum excluded Western subjects, much to the chagrin of reformers such as Prince Gong. See Daniel Barish, *Learning to Rule: Court Education and the Remaking of the Qing State, 1861–1912* (New York: Columbia University Press, 2022), 42–43.
8 See C. T. Hsia, *On Chinese Literature* (New York: Columbia University Press, 2004), 257.
9 Hsia, *On Chinese Literature*, 248.
10 See Luke S. K. Kwong, 'Self and Society in Modern China: Liu E (1857–1909) and Laocan youji', *T'oung Pao* 87.4-5 (2001), 360–392, here 373.
11 See Liu E (劉鶚), *The Travels of Lao Can*, trans. by Yang Xianyi and Gladys Yang (Beijing: Foreign Language Press, 2005).
12 Liu, *The Travels*, 119–120.
13 See Xiangjun Feng, '*The Travels of Lao Can* as a Book of Prophecy', *Journal of the Royal Asiatic Society* 33 (3034), 203–228, here 215.
14 For a complete list of the novel's continuations, see Hu Yannan (胡衍南), *Continuations of Dream of the Red Chamber: Research on Mid-Qing Secular Novels* (orig. 紅樓夢後—清代中期世情小說研究 Hong Lou Meng hou: Qingdai zhongqi shiqing xiaoshuo yanjiu) (Taipei: Wunan, 2022), 51–52.
15 Orig. '外國人的屎也是香的。只可惜我們沒福氣。不曾做了外國狗，吃他不著。' Wu Jianren (吳趼人), *Collected Works* (orig. 全集 Quan ji), 10 vols (Harbin: Beifang wenyi chubanshe, 1998), VI, 48. Henceforth quoted as NS.
16 Orig. '寶玉卻翻來覆去的睡不著，起來坐了一回，重復睡下。正要朦朧睡著，只見童子拿了一封信來，說道："來人立等回信。" [...] 寶玉問童子道："來人呢？" 童子道："在外面。" 寶玉起身到外面去，卻是黃福。黃福見了寶玉，便走前兩步，請了個安，道："敝上請老爺就到上海一轉，有要緊事。" 寶玉道："你等我僱了個飛車去。" 黃福道："不必飛車，已備馬在這裡了。" 寶玉看時，果然有兩匹馬在那裡，便跨上了馬，黃福也上馬相隨。撒開轡頭，那馬便追風逐電而去。過了幾處高山，歷盡許多荊棘，走到一處海邊，看見泊著一艘輪船。[...] 在海面上翻波踏浪的向前馳驟。寶玉大喜，也縱轡跟去，果然這匹馬也是一樣在海面上走。心中暗暗想道：從前聽見人說，千里馬渡水、登山如履平地，我只不信，原來是真正有的。 兩匹馬跑了許久，便到了上海。吳伯惠歡喜迎接，說了好些別後的話，寶玉便問有甚麼緊要的事，伯惠笑道："並沒有要緊事，不過許久不見了，請你來會會談談，並且同你去各處遊歷。" 寶玉道："我自從到了文明境界，一切都漢觀止了，再遊歷甚麼呢？" 伯惠道："你原來不知道，自從你走了之後，出了好些新聞。兩宮回鑾之後，次第舉行新政，一切都同戊戌那年差不多。不過戊戌那年是雷厲風行，這回是慢騰騰的舉動，所以不甚見效。忽然為了美國人禁止華人入境的約，到了改約之期，中國商界、學界的人 [...] 相戒不用美貨。由上海倡起，各省各埠一齊嚮應 [...] 。這事傳到了北京，政府裡聽見這個消息，便知道中國民氣可用。'[...] 俯仰之間，覓得身子在輪船上，那輪船走的十分快捷。看看兩岸，全是高大房屋，煙囪如林，不覺自言自語道："這是那裡呢？向來沒有到過。" 忽聽得伯惠在背後道："這裡是揚子江呀！" 寶玉回頭問道："長江兩面，那裡有許多房屋？" 伯惠道："你還不知道呢？此刻從吳淞起，一直到漢口，兩岸全是中國廠家，接連不斷的了。"'(NS 310–317).

17 Orig. '一轉眼間，船已到了漢口。[...] 抬頭一看，路旁一所極大的房子，房子前面一片空場。空場上豎了一枝插天高的旗桿，掛著一面飛龍黃旗，迎風招展。另外有一根長繩，[...] 沿繩掛著五洲萬國的國旗。看那房子門口時，鑿了〉萬國和平會〈 五個字，都用飛金鋪了，映著日光，十分耀目。寶玉便踱了進去，只見裡面設了一個大會場，中國、外國的人坐滿場上，也不知有多少人。坐了半天，還是寂寂無聲。忽聽得一陣鈴向，耳邊有人悄悄的說道："主席的上臺了，這便是中國皇帝。" [...] 忙向臺上看時，講席上站著的卻是東方文明，演說道："今日萬國和平會開會之第一日，蒙各國公舉朕為會長。 [...] 此和平會當為全球人類求和平，而各國政府，當擔負其保護和平之責任。如紅色種、黑色種、棕色種，各種人均當平等相待，不得凌虐其政府及其國民。[...] 對於此等無知識之人，均有誘掖教育之責任。[...] 故自此次開會之後，當消滅強權主義，實行和平主義。" 合場上下一齊鼓掌。寶玉鼓掌不已，又要頓足。誰知一頓足，卻腳踏了空，一落千丈，兩眼登時昏黑，嚇的一身冷汗。勉強睜開雙眼看時，原來還睡在東方文明家裡客房裡面的牀上，竟是一場大夢。'(NS 310–325).

18 See Frank Dikötter, *The Discourse on Race in Modern China* (Oxford: Oxford University Press, 2015), 37–60.
19 See David Der-wei Wang, *Fin-de-siècle Splendor: Repressed Modernities of Late Qing Fiction, 1849–1911* (Stanford: Stanford University Press, 1997), 283.
20 Analyses of Chinese contemporary politics frequently address the nexus between Xi Jinping's Chinese Dream and ancient ideas of how power is legitimized. See Lanxin Xiang, 'Introduction: Legitimacy–East and West', in: *The Quest for Legitimacy in Chinese Politics*, ed. by L. X. (London: Routledge, 2019), 1–8.
21 Xi's personal account of the Cultural Revolution has been made into a book, *Xi Jinping's Seven Years as a Zhiqing* (習近平的七年知青歲月, 2017). As Xu Bin argues, his apotheosis overshadows the memories of 17 million fellow citizens. See Xu Bin, *Chairman Mao's Children: Generation and the Politics of Memory in China* (Cambridge University Press, 2021), 2.
22 Ma Jian (馬建), *China Dream*, trans. by Flora Drew (London: Chatto, 2020), 11. Henceforth quoted as CD.
23 Georg Lukács, *The Theory of the Novel*, trans. by Anna Bostock (Cambridge, MA: MIT Press, 1971), 66.

Bibliography

Barish, Daniel. *Learning to Rule: Court Education and the Remaking of the Qing State, 1861–1912* (New York: Columbia University Press, 2022).
Benite, Zvi Ben-Dor. 'Long Divided Must Unite, Long United Must Divide: Dynasty, Histories, and the Orders of Time in China', in: *Power and Time: Temporalities in Conflict and the Making of History*, ed. by Dan Edelstein et al. (Chicago: University of Chicago Pres, 2020), 147–173.
Dikötter, Frank. *The Discourse on Race in Modern China* (Oxford: Oxford University Press, 2015).
Feng, Xiangjun. '*The Travels of Lao Can* as a Book of Prophecy', *Journal of the Royal Asiatic Society* 33 (3034), 203–228.
Hsia, C. T. *On Chinese Literature* (New York: Columbia University Press, 2004).
Hsün Tzu (=Xunzi 荀子). *Basic Writings*, trans. by Burton Watson (New York: Columbia University Press, 1969).
Hu, Yannan (胡衍南). *Continuations of Dream of the Red Chamber: Research on Mid-Qing Secular Novels* (orig. 紅樓夢後—清代中期世情小說研究 Hong Lou Meng hou: Qingdai zhongqi shiqing xiaoshuo yanjiu) (Taipei: Wunan, 2022).
Kwong, Luke S. K. 'Self and Society in Modern China: Liu E (1857–1909) and Laocan youji', *T'oung Pao* 87.4-5 (2001), 360–392.
Legge, James (ed.). *The Sacred Books of China: The Texts of Confucianism*, trans. by J. L., 2 vols (Oxford: Clarendon Press, 1879).
Liu E (劉鶚). *The Travels of Lao Can*, trans. by Yang Xianyi and Gladys Yang (Beijing: Foreign Language Press, 2005).
Liu, T'ieh-yün (劉鐵雲) (=Liu E). *The Travels of Lao Ts'an*, trans. by Harold Shadick (Ithaca, NY: Cornell University Press, 1952).
Lukács, Georg. *The Theory of the Novel*, trans. by Anna Bostock (Cambridge, MA: MIT Press, 1971).
Ma, Jian (馬建). *China Dream*, trans. by Flora Drew (London: Chatto, 2020).
Needham, Joseph. *The Shorter Science and Civilisation in China*, 5 vols (Cambridge University Press, 1980–1995).
Wang, David Der-wei. *Fin-de-siècle Splendor: Repressed Modernities of Late Qing Fiction, 1849–1911* (Stanford: Stanford University Press, 1997).
Wu, Jianren (吳趼人). *Collected Works* (orig. 全集 Quan ji), 10 vols (Harbin: Beifang wenyi chubanshe, 1998).
Xiang, Lanxin (ed.). *The Quest for Legitimacy in Chinese Politics* (London: Routledge, 2019).
Xu, Bin. *Chairman Mao's Children: Generation and the Politics of Memory in China* (Cambridge University Press, 2021).

Index

Note: Endnotes are indicated by the page number followed by 'n' and the endnote number e.g., 20n1 refers to endnote 1 on page 20.

Account of the World Inside a Pillow (枕中記) 30
alcoholic intoxication 21, 47, 49, 52, 91–2
Analects of Confucius (論語) 4–5, 12n11
anthropomorphism 11, 35, 51

Book of Changes (易經) 2, 4
Book of Documents (書經) 91
Boundless Night (茫茫夜) 64, 78–9
Buber, Martin 7
Buddhism 7, 11, 29–31, 35–6, 47, 51, 65–6, 72–3, 83
butterfly dream 5–8, 11, 34, 84

Cao, Xueqin (曹雪芹) 31, 64, 70, 98
Caramel Girl (卡爾美夢姑娘) 64–5, 79–82
Carnal Prayer Mat (肉蒲團) 65–70, 72, 83
China Dream (novel) (中國夢) 90, 102–8
Chinese Communist Party 103, 106
'Chinese Dream' (political formula) 90, 107–8
Chinese mythology 4, 51–2, 55, 94, 99, 102, 106–7
Chinese nationalism 84, 98–100, 107–8

Christianity 64, 73, 77–9, 83, 90, 95–6
chuanqi (傳奇) 50, 58, 60n11
Classic of Mountains and Seas (山海經) 43
Classic of Poetry (詩經) 2, 22–3, 39–40n16, 46–7, 91
'clouds and rain' (雲雨) 26, 71, 73
colonial aggression 95–6, 98, 100–1
Commentary of Zuo (左傳) 57, 73
Confucianism 3–5, 12n10, 20, 39, 46, 73, 94–5, 108n7
Confucius (孔子) 4–5, 7–8, 11, 13n11, 39n14, 46, 71, 73
Continuation of Plum in the Golden Vase (續金瓶梅) 21–2, 53
cosmos 3, 7, 51, 84, 91
Cultural Revolution (文化大革命) 103–5, 110

Dao De Jing (道德經) 6
Daoism 6–9, 11, 30–1, 34–6, 39, 47, 51, 65, 68, 72–3, 94, 108
Ding, Yaokang (丁耀亢) 21, 53
divination 1–4
Doctrine of the Mean (中庸之道) 69–70
doppelgänger 32–4, 37–8
dream interpretation: by the Emperor 26; literal 5; by mancers

2–3, 45, 47; popular 5, 13n18; by scholars 3–4, 6–7, 29–30, 36–7, 50, 91
Dream of the Red Chamber (紅樓夢) 18, 31–8, 70–4, 83–4, 98, 101
Dream of the Southern Branch (play) (南柯記) 51
dreams: ancestral 1, 5, 20, 70–1, 83; classification of 1; gendered 46; medical aspects of 21–2, 64, 73–4, 83; as metaphors 22, 70, 94–5, 103; sexual and erotic 24, 24–5, 64–89; social stratification of 3, 5, 37, 46; 'strange' 1, 5, 35, 38, 54; symbolic 2, 5, 13n18, 45–6, 70; prophetic 1–4, 5, 11, 45–7, 58, 70, 91, 97, 106
Duke of Zhou (周公) 4–5, 8, 11, 13n13, 22

Emperor Qianlong (乾隆) 44
Empress Cixi (慈禧) 95, 100
Empress Wu Zetian (武則天) 83
escapism 8, 36, 50
Extensive Records of the Taiping Era (太平廣記) 44, 46–7, 59, 59n7

foxes (狐狸精) 43, 51–9, 61n17
Freud, Sigmund 65, 74, 77, 79, 83, 85–6n13, 106

Gan, Bao (干寶) 44–5
Garden of the Extraordinary (異苑) 44
genre 43–4, 58–9, 62n29
Giles, Herbert 7
Goethe, Johann Wolfgang 78, 85n9
gothic horror 79, 82
Governor of Nanke (南柯太守傳) 43, 47–51, 55, 58–9
Greek mythology 79, 83
Guo, Moruo (郭沫若) 64–5, 75, 77–84
Guo, Xiang (郭象) 6–7

Han dynasty (漢朝) 12–13n11, 43
Hanshan, Deqing (憨山德清) 7

Health Benefits of the Bedchamber (房中補益) 74
homosexuality 66, 75–6, 84
Hu, Shi (胡適) 37
Hundred-Days-Reform (戊戌變法) 95, 99

In Search of the Supernatural (搜神記) 44–6

Jia, Baoyu (賈寶玉) 31–8, 70–4, 83–4, 98–103
Jin, Shengtan (金聖歎) 29–30, 35, 36–7

karma and retribution 18, 34, 65, 68–9

Late Spring (殘春) 82–4
Leibniz, Gottfried-Wilhelm 12n10
Li, Yu (李漁) 64–5, 69–70
Li, Gongzuo (李公佐) 43, 50
Liang, Qichao (梁啟超) 95, 101
Liezi (列子) 8, 71, 91, 103, 107
Liu, E (劉鶚) 90, 91, 106–7
Liu, Xiang (劉向) 43
Lu, Xun (魯迅) 60n11, 82

Ma, Jian (馬建) 90, 102
Mandate of Heaven (天命) 11, 47, 91, 102
Mao, Zedong (毛澤東) 103
masturbation 66, 73, 76
medical views 3, 54–5, 64, 69, 73–4, 82–3, 106
Meiji period (Japan) 77, 94–5
Mencius (孟子) 22, 31, 71, 73
mirrors 34, 105
Moving South (南遷) 64, 75–7

nation state 90, 107
New Story of the Stone (新石頭記) 90, 98–102, 107
Nietzsche, Friedrich 77, 85–6n13

Peony Pavilion (牡丹亭) 17, 22–7, 31, 37, 76
People's Republic of China 90

Plum in the Golden Vase (金瓶梅) 17–20, 31, 37, 38n2
polygamy 20, 81
psychology (modern) 64, 74–7, 79, 83, 91, 106
Pu, Songling (蒲松齡) 43, 51, 59, 73

qi (氣) 5, 20, 74
Qing dynasty (清朝) 17, 29, 37, 43, 64–5, 75, 90–2, 94–8, 107

Records of the Grand Historian (史記) 3, 91
'red dust' (紅塵 hong chen) 47, 51
Reich, Wilhelm 77, 86n14
renunciation and asceticism 29–30, 35–6, 65–6, 68–9, 83
Rimbaud, Arthur 75
Romance of the Western Chamber (西廂記) 17, 27–31, 37–8
romantic love and *yuanfen* (緣分) 26–7, 37, 51, 75, 79, 81–2

Sade, Marquis de 70
satire 60n12, 68, 103, 105
scepticism 4, 57, 106
self-harm 68, 77, 83
sexual alchemy 54–5
sexual and erotic dreams 23, 24, 64–89; with ghosts 20–1, 53–5, 74
sexual explicitness, obscenity, and pornography 20–1, 23–4, 29, 64, 68, 70
Shen, Jiji (沈既濟) 30
Sinking (沈淪) 84
'slave mentality' 76–7, 79
Sōseki, Natsume 78
spirits, ghosts, and demons 4, 20–1, 26–8, 51, 54, 57–8, 61n17, 72–4, 76
spiritual salvation 30–1, 35–6, 44, 47, 51, 73, 83–4

Spring and Autumn Annals (呂氏春秋) 4
Story of Yingying (鶯鶯傳) 30
Strange Tales from a Chinese Studio (聊齋誌異) 43, 51–9, 73
suicide 65, 78, 81, 105

Tang, Xianzu (湯顯祖) 22, 51, 76
The Classic of Sunü (素女經) 55
Tian/Heaven (天) 11, 55, 91, 102, 107
Travels of Lao Can (老殘遊記) 90–7, 107
Treatise on Curiosities (博物誌) 44

utopian literature 97, 101

Verlaine, Paul 75
vernacular Chinese 17, 38n2, 65

Wang, Shifu (王實甫) 27, 31
Western dream concepts 57, 64, 74, 90, 108n1
wu (悟) 51, 60n9, 70
Wu, Jianren (吳趼人) 90, 98, 107

Xi, Jinping (習近平) 103–4, 107–8
xiaoshuo (小說) 17–18, 37, 38n2, 50, 60n11
Xunzi (荀子) 94

Yellow Emperor (黃帝) 8–9, 11, 71, 91, 103, 107
Yihetuan Movement (義和團) or Boxer Rebellion 91, 95
yin and *yang* (陰陽) 3, 46, 51, 55, 61n17, 64, 69, 73, 108
Yu, Dafu (郁達夫) 64, 74–9, 84

zhiguai (志怪) 43–63
Zhou dynasty (周朝) 1, 3, 13
Zhuangzi (莊子) 5–7, 11, 31, 34–5, 38, 44, 84

For Product Safety Concerns and Information please contact our EU representative GPSR@taylorandfrancis.com
Taylor & Francis Verlag GmbH, Kaufingerstraße 24, 80331 München, Germany

www.ingramcontent.com/pod-product-compliance
Lightning Source LLC
Chambersburg PA
CBHW051753230426
43670CB00012B/2267